Saving Work

Saving Work

FEMINIST PRACTICES OF THEOLOGICAL EDUCATION

Rebecca S. Chopp

Westminster John Knox Press
Louisville, Kentucky

Grateful acknowledgment is made to Alfred A. Knopf, Inc., for permission to reprint lines from "Rape poem," from *Circles on the Water,* by Marge Piercy, copyright © 1982 by Marge Piercy.

Book and cover design by Drew Stevens

First edition

Published by Westminster John Knox Press
Louisville, Kentucky

This book is printed on acid-free paper that meets the American National Standards Institute Z39.48 standard. ∞

PRINTED IN THE UNITED STATES OF AMERICA

95 96 97 98 99 00 01 02 03 04 — 10 9 8 7 6 5 4 3 2 1

Library of Congress Cataloging-in-Publication Data

Chopp, Rebecca S., date.
  Saving work : feminist practices of theological education /
      p.   cm.
  Includes bibliographical references.
  ISBN 0-664-25539-6 (alk. paper)
    1. Theology—Study and teaching. 2. Women clergy—Training of.
  3. Feminist theology.   I. Title.
  BV4020.C48   1995
  230'.07—dc20   94-36761

Dedicated to Kathleen Yeager,
sister and friend,
who has taught me many things
about women and saving work

Contents

Preface

One of the most significant changes in theological education in the last twenty years has been the dramatic rise in the number of women students. In some theological schools women make up more than 50 percent of the student body. In addition, the emergence of feminist theologies provides new discourses about women's lives, the nature of Christianity, and the substance of theology. For many women and some men, participation in feminist classes, feminist spirituality groups, feminist liturgies, and women's caucuses constitutes the formative basis of their theological education. The presence of women, the emergence of feminist theology, and the production of new religious practices represent the emergence of what I call feminist liberationist Christianity within theological education. While previous books and articles have identified the struggles women face in theological education and the goals of theological education within feminist theology, there has been, as yet, no systematic interpretation of feminist practices of theological education.

At the same time that women have been entering theological education in massive numbers, a great deal of literature has been written on the present "crisis" of theological education. Much of my research in the last seven years has focused on this writing. I was asked some years ago to contribute to an evaluation of this literature from the perspective of "younger scholars." As I traveled around the United States consulting with younger scholars, I realized that although much of this literature is interesting and important, none of it considers the changes in theological education brought about by the presence of women and the emergence of feminist practices within theological education.

Several years ago I was asked by Jim Waits to write a book on emergent trends in theological education as part of a project he was

directing on the future of university-related divinity schools. The gen-
erosity of the project and the support of Jim Waits allowed me to host
several consultations on the future of theological education. These
consultations were designed to bring new voices and new perspectives into the discussions on theological education. Through these
consultations I became convinced of the need to develop a new
method of reflection on theological education that attended to cultural
movements and actual practices within theological education, based
on the current subjects (the students) of theological education.

After several failed attempts to write a book on the future of
theological education, I discovered that I could not write a kind
of universal perspective on the future of theological education, or
even on theological education in university-related divinity schools.
At this point, at least in my judgment, what is needed are analyses
from the perspectives of particular groups within theological education. Because I have been engaged in the feminist movement within
theological education for at least twenty years, I decided to focus on
women engaged in feminist practices of theological education in
order to speak about one cultural group within theological education. Of course, my view is only partial, since no one can ever hope
to describe the whole of feminist practices, let alone present the en-
tirety of what goes on for women in theological education.

I have written this book with three intentions. First, I hope this
book can serve as a useful resource for women and men who participate in feminist practices of theological education. I realize, of
course, that not all women identify themselves as feminists. I also
recognize that some men actively engage in feminist practices of theological education. Many women and some men selectively participate in feminist practices of theological education. Nonetheless,
actual practices of feminist theological education influence, even if
only by way of resistance, almost all women and men engaged in
theological education. I hope this book can serve as some type of
guide to what the present and future of feminist practices of theological education offer.

I also hope this book may invite a kind of "second generation"
of research in theological education that is sensitive to issues of particularity and contextuality as it exists within theological education.
Although much of the "first generation" literature has addressed
general problems of pluralism and fragmentation for one particular
understanding of knowledge, there has been no sustained effort to
reflect on pluralism of different Christian movements and cultures
within theological education. Before we can move forward to speak

about general aims of theological education, I think we must speak about specific practices and particular subjects.

I have constructed a method to identify and reflect on feminist practices of theological education. This is simply an initial statement about such practices. I hope my method will model for others a way to reflect on specific practices and particular subjects from their own perspectives. Even if my model only encourages resistance and critique, my third hope for this book will be met if it stimulates conversation about particularity and contextuality within theological education.

This book begins by tracing the presence of women in theological education, the construction of feminist scholarship, and the present status of reflection on theological education. I argue for the necessity of reflection on feminist practices of theological education, defining the notion of practices and specifying how ideas work within such feminist practices of theological education. In chapter 1 I examine three basic practices of narrativity, ekklesiality (the feminist construction of church), and theology in feminist theological education. The second chapter focuses on the practice of narrativity in terms of how women use theological education to compose or write new narratives for their lives. The third chapter concentrates on ekklesiality in terms of how feminist practices of church become constructed around the theological symbols of sin and grace. The fourth chapter considers the construction of feminist theology as a saving work formed through what I call a pragmatic critical theory. In chapter 5, I conclude with a partial vision of feminist theological education based on the themes of justice, dialogue, and imagination.

This book has numerous limiting factors. First, I have limited it to claims about "mainline" schools of theological education in the United States. While I have had the privilege of visiting schools in Canada, I think that the cultural situation of Canada is different enough to merit separate attention. Second, since my own background is in theological education in mainline schools, including those not specifically denominationally based, I have attempted only to interpret what I see in schools I know. An interesting project would be to study what goes on for women in schools related to evangelical movements in the United States and for women in para-institutions of theological education. The third limitation exists within my training as a systematic theologian and the kinds of questions I ask. I tend to ask questions about what practices mean to persons and how the symbols involved relate to activities produced.

Acknowledgments of gratitude are almost endless in this book.

I need to thank, first of all, the many women, and men, who participate in feminist practices of theological education. I hope I have spoken faithfully of your experience. (Stories told here are indirectly
modeled on actual stories. Names of persons, however, have been
changed.) I also want to thank Jim Waits and the advisory board of
the Future of University-Related Divinity Schools Project for their
encouragement in relation to this volume. I want to thank the Lilly
Foundation for its support of the Future of University-Related
Divinity Schools Project. I want also to thank persons who have
worked with me in various consultations and conversations: Sharon
Welch, Mark Lewis Taylor, Thomas Thangaraj, Vincent Wimbush,
Barbara Wheeler, Adele Collins, Mary McClintock Fulkerson, Robert
Franklin, Valerie De Marinis, Francis Schüssler Fiorenza, Catherine
Keller, Mary Elizabeth Moore, Kathryn Tanner, Edward Farley, Joe
Hough, Peter Hodgson, Don Browning, and David Kelsey. Charles
Foster, Pamela Couture, Roberta Bondi, Nancy Ammerman, Brooks
Holifield, Gene Tucker, Thomas Frank, Gail O'Day, and Gary Mey-
ers, all colleagues of mine at Emory, have patiently listened and gra-
ciously contributed to this volume. Friends who have provided me
with suggestions, support, and encouragement include Susan
Shapiro, Eliza Ellison, Mel Lockhart, Millie Feske, Mary Ann Zim-
mer, Will Coleman, Don Compier, Pamela Hall, Alicia Frank, Pam
Johnson, and Fred Thibodeau. I want also to thank my son, Nate
Biddle, my brother, Tom Chopp, and my parents, Delbert and Marion
Chopp, for their continued presence in my life and their interest in
my writing projects. This book is dedicated to my sister, Kathleen
Yeager, who has in so many ways contributed to practices of sur-
vival and flourishing in my life, and, consistently and patiently,
taught me the values of saving work.

1. Women as Subjects of Theological Education?

The class in feminist theology was three hours long, with two thirds of the time devoted to a critical reading of the night's text and the last third devoted to some kind of appropriation of the material. As I did every semester, I approached this first evening of class with a pedagogy based on textual explanation, critical analysis, and creative imagining and with a great deal of apprehension. What if we couldn't combine explanation, critique, and imaginative construction? Why didn't I direct all the discussion, by which I could quickly and easily keep control of the class and decide what was to be learned? Why try this balance of communal and individual learning, this combination of imaginative, aesthetic, and ordered, cognitive learning?

We read Rosemary Radford Ruether's *Sexism and God-Talk*.[1] The class was struggling with naming the pain of patriarchy and with visualizing hope. It was obvious to the students that this naming the depth of brokenness while at the same time announcing new possibilities was a Christian enterprise. This juxtaposition of brokenness and hope, of pain and new life, was what they had heard, in a variety of ways, throughout their Christian lives and certainly throughout most of their seminary education.

As we returned from break to participate in a student-led discussion section, we found the chairs placed in a circle. A wooden cross stood in the middle of the room. The women leading this part of the class session handed each of us a slip of paper as we entered and asked us to write down one specific experience of patriarchal oppression. As we sat in our circle around the cross, one by one we took turns naming each of these acts of patriarchy. Some women and men named experiences of individual pain, many of them acts of violence or acts of silencing. Others spoke about a woman or a man

they loved who had been hurt by patriarchy, while still others
named patriarchal acts affecting large groups of women. After each
one read aloud the sin inscribed on the paper, she or he nailed the
paper to the cross.

After a prayer, a table (altar) was uncovered. On it were all sorts
of things. One by one we chose from this array, which included a
kaleidoscope, a sand dollar, a bowl, a goddess image, a mask, an In-
dian doll, a Brazilian wood carving, a glass statue, a wreath, a rock,
a gourd, a shell. Then again we spoke, this time about new possibilities of God through the use of the symbols we had chosen. A
woman spoke of the kaleidoscope as imaging the changing patterns
of God in her life; another woman spoke of the fruit she had chosen
as representing life-giving forces in her experience; still another
spoke of the wreath as a symbol of eternal, creative presence.

This educational and liturgical memory is always with me when
I think about "theological education." It represents, at least for me, education as a process of spiritual and ecclesial formation that is focused
in and through theological wisdom. This event symbolizes those
times when all that I have read about theological education comes together with the concrete promise of students engaged in theological
education. This liturgy of healing and hope reminds me of the power
of persons to make new life, including new forms of theological education, out of what may appear dead bones or empty forms.

In classes, in hallways, in women's caucus meetings, in worship,
in spirituality groups, feminists are developing their own forms of
theological education. This book is about naming and describing
these forms, which exist within many of our schools. These forms of
feminist theological education receive little sustained attention in
scholarly works in theological education and are literally not seen
by many faculty and administrators or by some students.

Yet to name the power and presence of women (and men) engaged in feminist practices of theological education is to be able to
hear deep spiritual powers of transformation in the very midst of
the schools so many of us find in crisis. The women and men who
participated in the liturgy that night represent a significant movement of hope and a powerful source of joy for us in theological education and Christianity.

This book addresses how we might see and speak about the reality of women and men engaged in the practices of feminist theological education: in classes, in worship, in spirituality groups, in
individual lives. The central thesis of this book is that feminist theology provides us resources to name, in our midst, the powerful re-

ality of women and men transforming and being transformed in theological education through the practices of narrativity, ekklesiality, and theology. Implicit in my thesis is that such feminist practices, along with other contemporary Christian movements in theological education, provide the material for the concrete realization of the basic ideas that the recent generation of writers on theological education have developed.

As books inevitably are, this one is deeply woven with my life. My adult years have been spent as a participant in theological education and run parallel with the tremendous influx of women in theological education in the last twenty years. During these years, my perception and analysis of the presence of women in theological education have shifted through the spectrum of positions. Entering St. Paul School of Theology in Kansas City, Missouri, in 1973, I was hardly a liberal feminist, having been unexposed both to women in ministry and to feminist literature! For me, as for my local church and district boards of ministry, women who entered the ministry fell under the category of "exceptions." As time went on, and my knowledge of Christianity developed and my experiences as a woman in theological education and in the ordained ministry included both positive and negative elements, I developed a view of women in theological education through corrective and complementary views: women helped even the balance, so to speak, and women added new perspectives and styles.

Like many women, even in those relatively "early" days of feminist presence in theological education, I participated in various groups focusing on women and Christianity. In Kansas City, the Women's Center for Theologizing offered women laity, ministers, and seminarians opportunities to reflect, to organize work in churches, and to share journeys, including our struggles, together. This wonderful group of women gave me space to explore and adopt various positions within feminist theology. Serving churches in Kansas, I began to realize more and more the depth and power of women's lives in the churches and how "church" itself could be understood quite differently from the position of women washing dishes after a potluck as compared to the position of men running the church business in the board meeting. In graduate school, I began to learn and realize the implications of the flexibility and historicality of Christianity, how tradition is, to quote one of my teachers, "a living object liable to growth and change."[2]

Through these years of education, I read avidly in feminist theology but wrote very little on the topic. In part, this was due to the

influence of some of my women colleagues and teachers who
warned me about what publishing in feminism would do to my career. But in part, it was due to my own need to first achieve a kind
of theoretical and symbolic richness in feminism and other contemporary emancipatory theories. As my confidence grew, I started to
write explicitly feminist theology as a way to participate in a religious and political project of freedom for all persons. Feminist theology and the feminist movement in Christianity came increasingly
to stand for the promise of good news for both women and men.
Following bell hooks, I came to understand feminism not as a set of
correct ideas or a fixed identity but as a movement in which I participate. As a movement, like many religious movements, Christian
feminism begins with the struggles and dreams of people in order to
anticipate transformation for all.

This book is written out of my own journey, as all books are
crafted out of the writer's life. It is written toward the horizon of
transformation of Christianity and theological education that I believe already exists, in an anticipatory fashion, in our midst. If we
can begin to name the possibilities for transformation that already
exist in the struggles and desires of movements such as feminism,
we will aid in continuing Christianity as a living presence, appropriate to the promise of its traditions and compatible with many of
the rich textures of contemporary experience. If we cannot awaken
to the possibilities in our midst, and find ways to anticipate transformations from the old to the new, then the present forms of theological education, despite all the excellent writings and conferences,
will become like religious paintings displayed in our museums.
Highly relevant and productive in their day, the various forms of art
hang on museum walls for persons to pass by and admire. Detached
from the political and religious struggles of the day, dead to producing existential emotions and guiding narratives, such art, at best,
gives us glimpses into life when religious practices of self, church,
and world produced energy and vision. Contemporary theological
education may well be headed toward a destiny like that of such
past forms of religious art—simply to be observed and catalogued as
a part of history.

For those who find it hard to believe that in feminism and other
contemporary Christian movements reside the promise and material of transformation, it may be helpful to remember that one of the
consistent ironies of religious history in the United States is that institutions, practices, cultural formations, and ideas intended for one
objective sometimes get used in quite different ways. In the classic

text *From Sacred to Profane America,* William A. Clebsch identifies how American religious movements repeatedly produced effects of transformation they did not intend.[3] Early American settlers came under the guise of piety to establish the city of God, and what resulted were the cities of man. Though we might today take issue with the ways Clebsch frames his story, the irony of religion as practiced is important to recall: deep in the patterns of historical life, religious practices, including religious ideas, often take new forms and shapes.

I am convinced that feminist practices of theological education hold great promise for the future of theological education. This does not mean I think that feminism has all the answers or will supply some comprehensive unity for all issues in theological education. Indeed, it is the pluralism of the many movements within contemporary theological education in which the promise of the future resides. Feminism will contribute its practices, including new symbols and ideas, along with contributions from other movements. As this chapter will seek to demonstrate, feminism will help provide the concrete data of practices and theological *habitus,* which has been identified as the goal of transformation in recent writings on theological education. For what finally will prevent present-day theological education from becoming like the art on our museum walls is the saving work in which women and men are already engaged through feminist practices of theological education.

The Situation

For at least twenty-five years, feminism has offered its resources in North American schools of theological education. The contributions feminism has made in theological education in this period can readily be listed. Yet feminist scholars are among the first to wonder whether or not these contributions have made a difference, or, more accurately, if feminism has had any significant impact on the structure of theological education.

We can begin by listing, in quite an abbreviated form, the contributions feminism has made to theological education. Certainly, the presence of large numbers of women in theological education has feminist implications because significant numbers provide a critical mass to start questioning the ideological assumptions about women and the relations between the sexes. The increasing presence of women scholars provides not only much-needed role models but persons doing research on the neglected or repressed areas of women and the Bible, women in church history, feminist ethics, and so on. The presence of women, then, both as scholars and as students, provides the context for the following contributions of feminism in theological education.

The Uncovering of New Voices and Faces in History

Tremendous work has been done on the role of women in history, including research into issues such as forgotten women leaders, overlooked religious movements among women, and biblical women long neglected. Such research not only provides new historical types of activity by selected persons in certain social positions but raises a question in historiography: How do we know the history of those who neither wrote nor read, who had neither a public voice nor a "significant" role in the military, the economic, the aesthetic, or the political production of history?

Defining New Areas of Research

What counts as valid research is generally related to the concerns and issues of the day. An acceptable area of research in the present situation encompasses the numerous issues related to women. Admissible research now includes topics such as how gender is represented in theological texts or how popular religion is always gendered as feminine in academic literature.

New Resources, New Models

Research on women's experiences has provided us with new models and images of God, community, Christology, and spirituality. These images and models have often fit into contemporary forms of theology, emphasizing God as more loving (more feminine), the church as more caring (more like a family), or even spirituality as more earthly (bodily, like a woman). But increasingly, feminists are questioning the very genre of contemporary theology by seeking to discover new forms of theological reflection.

Inclusive Language

Feminism has had some fair success with insisting on inclusive language, either in the form of substituting nongendered terms for God and humanity or in the form of including feminine terms for God and humanity. Some schools and many journals have policies requiring inclusive language for all writing. Although debates still rage about whether or not one can change the scriptures, other use of inclusive language seems to be a fairly standard practice.

These contributions are important and, given the brief history of women in theological education, impressive. Many of us can remember when women, as a rule, were told not to ruin their careers in the academy and the church by being too connected to feminism or women's concerns. Today in many schools, women and men can study feminism and in some of our schools are required to study feminism—that signifies major changes in a very brief span of time.

But such applause has to be quickly modulated, for feminists still find themselves and their issues marginalized. Indeed, after making a close survey of material and persons related to feminism and theological education, one wonders whether feminism has a significant voice at all in theological education. In 1980 the Cornwall Collective, composed of women who were working in ongoing projects within theological education, published a book titled *Your Daughters Shall Prophesy: Feminist Alternatives in Theological Education*, outlining feminist criticisms of theological education and proposing some basic revisions, including some alternative forms of theological education.[4] Yet in spite of, or perhaps because of, their projects and their years in theological education, they could say: "Questions raised by women, blacks, Hispanics, Native Americans, and the poor are seen as peripheral."[5] The Cornwall Collective criticized theological education for its division of theory and practice, its organization of disciplines, its reliance on claims of "objectivity," and its use of the model of university education, which lack any concern for integration or spirituality. Relying on the resources of women in theological education, the Cornwall Collective called for theological education to be more holistic, more aware of its political nature, more community oriented. Five years later, the Mud Flower Collective produced *God's Fierce Whimsy*, a book dedicated to trying to "help" theological education, because the authors of the book found that Christian seminaries are "arenas in which lukewarm faith and uninspired scholarship are peddled."[6] The Mud Flower Collective offers much the same analysis of theological education as does the Cornwall Collective: "Since the early 1970's the number of women students in U.S. seminaries has increased 222%. During this period of time, structural changes in seminaries have been minimal."[7]

Indeed, the difference between the 1980 Cornwall Collective and the 1985 Mud Flower Collective could be interpreted as revealing increased frustration at the inability to get feminist issues heard within theological education. The Mud Flower Collective declares that, first and foremost, its text is written to reach other feminist women in theological education who, "As players with us in the grandiose games of misogynist academic gymnastics . . . have been involved in a lose-lose situation."[8]

This increased frustration identifies as problematic the very same issues that the Cornwall Collective found prohibitive to good theological education. The Mud Flower Collective cites such issues as the politics of education, the role of cultural pluralism, the standards of excellence, the relation of theory and praxis, the role of community, the claims of validity in scholarship, and the structure of theological reflection as the problems for women in theological education. The problems of women and for women in theological education are not merely women's historical lack of participation, but how theological education is defined, formed, and structured. Once a critical mass of women appear in theological education, problems of the structure, purpose, and nature of theological education become more and more evident.

Writings on Theological Education

At approximately the same time as large numbers of women entered theological education, theologians began to lament the crisis in theological education. Edward Farley in *Theologia*, the landmark document in recent studies in theological education, sets the tone by titling his introduction "The Travail of the Theological School."[9] Joseph Hough and John Cobb in *Christian Identity and Theological Education* begin with the sentence, "*Anyone* associated with theological education for ministers in the 'main-line' Protestant churches of the United States is surely aware that there is widespread discontent with the schools providing this education."[10] Max Stackhouse in *Apologia* makes the explicit observation, "Modern theological education, perhaps especially in ecumenically oriented seminaries, is in a severe crisis even where it is carried on with some 'success.'"[11] Though the authors never really describe this crisis, all begin their works with some analysis or characterization of what lies behind the crisis, naming such issues as the current organization of the curriculum, the lack of Christian identity, and/or the confusion of theory and praxis.

Though several of the authors do cite factors of institutionality, culture, and religion as contributing to the crisis in theological education, most of the authors choose to focus their work on ideational issues of self-identity. By self-identity I mean the attempt to figure out what theological study is in its own terms, especially focusing on an ideal pattern that allows continuity and security amid different contexts, applications, and options. The basic approach of those grappling with the crisis of theological education is to get the idea of theological education correct, to understand appropriately and adequately the idea of theological education before one turns to the subjects, to the reality of church, and to patterns of Christian symbolic practice. If the ideal aim of theological education can be articulated, then the power of that idea will shape and direct all other concerns.

In *Theologia*, Edward Farley argues against the specialization of disciplines, the technical transformation of knowledge into strategic "know-how" techniques, and the clericalization of theological education.[12] These factors, among others, banish the classical sense of *habitus*, or theology as wisdom and science. Since *habitus* provides the unity and the rationale of the theological enterprise, theological education needs to restore *theologia* to theological education. In his constructive position, Farley calls for theological education to be reformed around a recovery of *theologia* as a reflective wisdom of faith. In his second book, *The Fragility of Knowledge*, Farley continues the critique of modern structures of knowledge of religion, arguing that some type of *habitus* is essential to knowledge, as it is to faith itself.[13] In this text, Farley argues that the hermeneutical principles must follow the nature of the religion. Farley contends: "I have described religion as making a reality claim concerning the widest context of experience, as presupposing and shaping human experience in distinctive ways, and as socially and historically concrete. These features undergird three hermeneutical principles for the study and teaching of religion: principles of concreteness, experientiality, and reality."[14]

In his book *To Understand God Truly*, David Kelsey turns his attention to issues parallel to those expressed in Farley's three hermeneutical principles.[15] Kelsey attempts to deal with the concreteness of all the diverse forms of theological education by finding a unity based on the ideal of the common goal of understanding God more truly. Recognizing all the differences among various theological schools as true to the reality of knowing God, Kelsey calls us to understand theological schools and Christian congregations through the concreteness of their practices. Arguing that it is impossible to restore *habitus* in the sense of moving back behind the modern structure of knowledge as *Wissenschaft*, or critical, orderly, disciplined research, Kelsey suggests a new relationship between *habitus* and *Wissenschaft*. By formulating the goal of knowledge as a *habitus*, Kelsey suggests that we might "capacitate" students "as agents in a shared public world to apprehend God Christianly" by "using the *range* of things studied and the type of *critical thinking* employed" appropriated for the *Wissenschaft* model.[16]

To a surprising extent, the problems raised by Farley and Kelsey are almost the same as those raised by the feminist writings on theological education. Without giving explicit attention to feminist reflection on theological education, Farley and Kelsey focus on the same issues of fragmentation, validity claims in theology, theory and praxis, and lack of integration. Farley, for instance, in *Theologia* and in *The Fragility of Knowledge,* comes quite close to many of the feminist concerns as he criticizes the present organization of studies and as he conceives the structure of theological study, calling for a *habitus* that the Cornwall Collective might describe as holistic.

Yet researchers in theological education have not yet paid attention to feminism as a resource for the critique and transformation of theological education. In *Theologia* Farley suggests that feminism may be one of those forms of faith that contributes to a new *habitus*, but he does not use feminism as a resource in *The Fragility of Knowledge* for rethinking the structure of theological study. I want to suggest a distinct difference between the approach of feminists on issues of women in theological education and that of contemporary authors' writings from a general, and often abstract, perspective. For authors such as Farley and Kelsey, as well as for feminist theologians, the problems arise in the concreteness of reality. The problem of fragmentation that Farley addresses and the problem of pluralism that Kelsey considers arise out of the concreteness of present theological education. But for Farley and Kelsey the methodological strategies to understand and address the respective problems are aimed at discovering a unity above or beyond the fragmentation and pluralism.

The ideas of *theologia* in Farley's work and of "schooling" in

Kelsey's provide us with a kind of vision of what we lack and to which we aspire. But for both of these authors the constructive positions are formal, mediated neither through symbolic construction of faith nor through the particular subjects of theological education. The strategies of most of the work on theological education thus far are ideational, formulating an abstract ideal to offer some vantage point of unity amid the fragmentation and pluralism.

These are not unhelpful strategies, for Farley and Kelsey have provided us with a new vision of "knowledge," albeit in a very formal fashion, for theological education. But the formal nature of their strategies represents only one type of approach for addressing the crises of current theological education. Another strategy, and the one employed in this book, returns to the controversial issue of concreteness and attempts to discern the historical, cultural, and symbolic factors at work in present theological education. Using this more contextual approach, feminists investigate issues that concern women in theological education.

Rather than leave the matter at the ideational level of the work of writers such as Farley and Kelsey, the feminist investigation in this text asks questions in terms of investigating the concrete reality of contemporary theological education. What are the concrete practices in our midst: what symbols do they invoke, what virtues do they create, what ways of naming God do they entail? How are basic Christian practices being transformed in a time of dramatic cultural and personal change? How are the participants or subjects of theological education being formed through theological reflection and construction, being shaped in theological wisdom? What are the textures and contours of theological wisdom in this day and age? In this second generation of scholarship on theological education, we can take the ideas of Farley and Kelsey and use them to investigate the concrete data of our experiences in order to identify the struggles and desires for transformation as they exist in our midst.

What I am suggesting is that the second generation of literature on theological education needs to remake the formal method of the first generation of writers into practical methods that investigate contemporary reality—methods that can anticipate possibilities for transformation in our midst. In feminist theory, and other forms of contemporary theory, such refocusing of ideas falls under the general rubric known as "critical theories." A critical theory, according to feminist theorist Iris Young, is a theory that is historically and socially contextual. It does not attempt to make universal arguments or constructs that will hold for all times and places. A critical theory arises in a specific situation and, using the symbols, images, and concepts involved in that situation, attempts to move against distortion and dysfunction and to shape new forms of flourishing. Young explains, "Critical theory presupposes that the normative ideas used to criticize a society are rooted in experience and reflection on that society and that the norms can come from nowhere else."[17]

To develop such a contextual critical method, then, we must first return to the concrete. We must relocate our investigation from the abstract to the practical reality of our situation. In order to do this, we can foreground three factors: (1) who the subjects of theological education are; (2) the larger situation of cultural movements and changes; and (3) the symbolic patterns invoked in Christian practice.[18]

The first issue of contextual analysis can be phrased in a question: Who are the subjects of theological education? The recent works on theological education largely ignore the dramatic changes in the student body of theological education. Though there is occasional recognition in texts of the presence of women and blacks, almost all texts fail to consider the phenomenon of second-career students. Indeed, the books seem to assume, in new guise, a developmental model of education, one that has been adopted by the academy as appropriate for use with young adults but is largely unsuccessful for use with older students. In my own school, the subtext of developmental learning is a model of working through identity and authority issues in clinical placements in theological education. The identity and authority issues are those of young men in relation to older male authority figures, issues that no longer reflect the experience of many of our students. Indeed, given the wide diversity in our student body, it is hard to argue for one guiding anthropology to use in our educational model. The "modern" anthropological notion of the learner as an autonomous individual with a blank slate on which to impart knowledge no longer fits the reality of our students. Yet so far in the discussions of theological education, there has been little, if any, detailed attention to educational and anthropological theories that fit the current lives of our students, and the "modern" developmental notion of the autonomous individual continues to guide, if anonymously, the current writings on theological education.

In order to foreground the concrete reality of theological education, we must consider the present subjects of theological education. What does it matter that so many of our students are women (and, for other projects, second-career men)? What do these women want in theological education? Why do so many women say they come to seminary for opportunities for theological challenge and growth, and not necessarily to prepare for ordination?[19] Theological processes, as do all other cultural products, arise out of the persons who use them. A feminist approach to theological education begins by attending to the subjects and asking what is going on for them in theological education. In most, if not all, of the literature to date, the subjects of theological education are not mentioned. Education is not simply about correct ideas or handing down tradition or training in technical expertise; it is also about human change, transformation, growth. The "subjects" of theological education are the students.

The second issue of contextual analysis has to do with cultural movements and changes in the larger situation of U.S. culture. The bracketing of the larger cultural situation, including the university as a microcosm of culture, results in a failure to inquire into the material reality of the broader sociopolitical situation. Recent works in theological education by and large avoid any analysis of theological education in light of the larger cultural situation.[20] Even treatments of pluralism limit analysis to differences among theological schools. None of the works considered pluralism as a cultural phenomenon (for instance, the changing trends in religion in America, where large numbers of persons are evangelical Christians or New Age adherents). Likewise, none of the works really consider pluralism in a worldwide context or even world-religions context. The books don't even reflect on the pluralism within denominations, in which, as Robert Wuthnow has pointed out, denominations and churches have become "to a greater extent diverse federations of special purpose groups rather than monolithic, homogenous structures."[21]

One of the most interesting areas of neglect in recent writings on theological education is the importance of current religious movements affecting American culture in general and Christianity in particular. The reality of change and transformation being brought about by movements such as feminism is virtually ignored in this literature. And yet, in the history of Christianity significant changes have been brought about by movements that affect great change and transformation within and outside of the established church structures. Social theorists such as Raymond Williams and Anthony Giddens argue that in the contemporary situation, transformation will occur in culture in part due to the vitality and importance of such emergent or emancipatory movements.[22] Such movements will reclaim a selective reading of tradition, will reform cultural structures, and will offer new narratives and forms of practices. Like religious movements throughout history, these movements in our midst will likely become tomorrow's tradition to be debated, changed, and transformed.

The third issue of contextual analysis concerns an interpretation and construction of the symbolic patterns of Christian faith. The writings on theological education opt for a formal, theoretical analysis of the problem. Perhaps an example may suffice to begin to identify how these works fail to provide enough theological substance for feminist theology. Edward Farley argues that the unity of theological study ought to be conceived as *theologia*, a *habitus* of reflective learning. Farley is advocating an approach to theological study in which wisdom and knowledge are integrated.

From a feminist theological perspective, this language is, as we shall see, very helpful. But what is the body and flesh of this *habitus*? How does one talk of this concretely? For feminists the crisis of church, culture, and personal lives can be spoken of, in part, as the crisis of symbols, the crisis of meaning that produces transformation and encourages flourishing. The questions posed to theological education are not merely the questions of how knowledge, theoretically conceived, has become fractured, but also what symbols and narratives can best construct *habitus*. What do these symbols and narratives mean and how do they function in actual Christian praxis? Theologians have long known that symbols and narratives have to change and continually transform themselves if they are to be meaningful. The challenge is not simply to understand the formal goal of *habitus* but to develop a *habitus* of God or ecclesial redemption in this particular age. Farley gives recognition to this issue when he suggests that any formulation of *habitus* will in fact begin with an interpretation of ecclesia, faith as mediated through participation in redemptive community. The question, given Farley's recognition, then becomes, How does one construct such symbolic language within the present situation?

This third issue of contextual analysis relates to the first two because the interlocked crises of "different" subjects and new cultural movements in theological education entail a quest for new symbols, new narratives, and new figures of meaning and transformation. Perhaps the failure of theologians to do the work of symbolics—that is, to speak of God in our midst—is connected to their failure to read deeply the needs and desires of the culture. But the failure to offer symbolic visions is also related to what some have called the academic captivity of theological education. Theologians in recent years, living amid academic guilds, have become bound by a particular nature of academic theory in which method dominates. In what Terry Eagleton has called the "fetishization of criticism," academic theologians in recent years have enjoyed the debates about the theory of theology much more than the theology itself.[23] Debates about method have become more and more intense about smaller and smaller matters. When it is isolated from the striving and stresses of the culture and unattached from the context of the dreams and sufferings of actual human subjects, theology's material work with symbols runs dry. This detachment has serious consequences. For, again in Eagleton's insight, the social functions of such narrow attention to method alone deny the culture and subjects any symbolic engagement, any continual refashioning. The social function of such theological abstraction denies any genuine movement toward the future. The task is to name not only the sufferings and distortions but also the dreams and desires of the day. The goal is to name God in our midst through and in the concrete reality of present existence.

Transforming Practices

Standing within the concrete realities of students, cultural changes, and symbolic patterns, I want to use the idea of actual practices of theological education in order to see if the shape of *habitus*, or theological wisdom, emerges. In a parallel to work done in cultural anthropology, in cultural studies, and in the methods of contextual and practical theology, I want to examine how women and men actually use theological education to construct and participate in feminist practices of narrativity, ekklesiality, and theology. After this investigation, I will turn in the final chapter of this book to gather up the threads of how we might think about the emergence of *habitus* in and through these specific practices.

Before I begin, it may be helpful to define what I, following Kelsey and others, mean by practices. By the term *practice*, I mean socially shared forms of behavior that mediate between what are often called subjective and objective dimensions. A practice is a pattern of meaning and action that is both culturally constructed and individually instantiated. The notion of practice draws us to inquire into the shared activities of groups of persons that provide meaning and orientation to the world, and that guide action.

To focus on practices is a contemporary strategy within the broader turn to praxis and practical reason within contemporary critical theory. As in the term *praxis*, theorists use the term *practices* in somewhat different ways. Alasdair MacIntyre, for instance, speaks of practices as shared cooperative activities generative of internal goods guided by embedded standards of excellence.[24] For Michel Foucault, practices are the dispersions of power and knowledge that are neither subjective nor objective.[25] As different as these two definitions are, they share a common focus on the social construction of embedded patterns that produce both individual meaning and cultural organization.

In his writings on theological education, David Kelsey has suggested that theological education be organized around the study of concrete practices in congregations. Kelsey, relying heavily on MacIntyre, defines *practice* as

> any form of socially established cooperative human activity
> that is complex and internally coherent, is subject to standards
> of excellence that partly define it, and is done to some end but
> that does not necessarily have a product.[26]

As Kelsey suggests, practices are shared, they require interaction and mutual participation, and they are guided by norms or what he calls implicit rules. Craig Dykstra, another theologian who invokes the term *practices* in relation to the study of theological education, observes that practices are not individual techniques but shared activities through which knowledge—in its fullest sense—occurs.[27] Generally we learn practices through ongoing participation in a community. Worship, for instance, is a shared practice of the Christian faith in which Christians are formed and through which Christians interact with God and others. To express an idea about worship, such as reverence to God, does not fully capture the complex and rich pattern of actions, intentions, emotions, judgments, and meaning that constitute worship.

Kelsey is particularly clear in his analysis of practice on the stress of its *bodiliness*.[28] Though practices contain certain ideas, and the only way we can speak of practices is through ideas, practices themselves involve full embodied actions. Kelsey uses practices as a way to hold inner intention and outer behavior together, and thus to deny any systematic distinction between the spiritual/intellectual and the physical/material. For instance, as a practice, worship involves the movements of bodies, the sensorial engagement of sight, hearing, taste, smell, and feeling, and the involvements of affective, ethical, and cognitive dimensions of attentiveness. Viewing theology as a practice may allow us to interpret its communal nature, including understanding issues of where and how theology is done and by whom it is spoken and written. In sum, the *bodiliness* of practice allows a fuller sense of what goes on in the physical and temporal space of theological education.

One further comment on Kelsey's definition of *practice* is needed, and that has to do with practices as having a history and as being historically and socially relative. Practices, and the meanings they carry, are both bearers of "traditions" and, I would infer, the site of change and transformation. Indeed, the practices I have selected—narrativity, ekklesiality, and theology—are practices that are classical for many Christian traditions, including the so-called classical tradition of Western Christianity. Augustine wrote on these three practices throughout his life. Calvin, to select another Western classical author, has intertwined these three practices throughout his *Institutes.* Schleiermacher's collected corpus may well be considered the first rather thoroughgoing modern transformation of these three classical practices of Christianity. Given these traditions, it may not be surprising that today the practices of narrativity, ekklesiality, and theology are the site of contestation and transformation in Christianity and in theological education.

By focusing on practices, we engage the embeddedness and bodiliness of theological education as a way in which to name, if only in an anticipatory fashion, theological education as the formation of *habitus.* The *habitus* of theological education, as Craig Dykstra has suggested, is learned through participation in specific Christian practices.[29] *Habitus* involves ordered learning, not only of classical wisdom and of modern critical methods, but also of emotional, aesthetic, affectional, spatial, and empathetic learning.[30] In addition to ordered learning, *habitus* involves affections, judgments, perceptions, intentions, and bodily experiences and movements. Such a full notion of *habitus* will also require us to extend the range of concern for change in theological education beyond that of curriculum reform. Important as the ordering of our ideas are, education as *habitus* involves the formation of self and community as well as the reformulation of imaginative, aesthetic, and linguistic learning. As we shall see in the last chapter of this book, education must be discussed in terms of pedagogy, community building, and world dialogue. To limit ourselves to curriculum reform without asking other substantive questions about how we teach, what we teach, whom we teach, and where we teach is simply to keep rearranging and redecorating the deck furniture on an unsteady, if not already sinking, Titanic.

I begin my investigation into the concrete practices of feminist theological education by focusing on the practice of narrativity, a practice for which written testimony goes back at least as far as Augustine's *Confessions*. I do not mean to extend the modern focus on individualism by beginning with narrativity, but, in all fairness to most of the women interviewed for this book, the issue of narrativity is inescapable. The broadest way to conceive the problems to which feminism seeks to respond has to do with the dramatic change in the lives of women. One woman put it something like this: whether or not women choose to participate in feminist practices, they are engaged in the very nontraditional activity of going to seminary. There is no set discourse, no well-established narrative about the woman preacher, pastor, or priest. Her very presence requires narrativity.

I must also admit to an impression that leads me to put narrativity first, but I must qualify it as an unsubstantiated hunch. Many of the women who come to seminary transform their lives rather dramatically—representing an intensification of normal cultural upheaval about women. During more than thirteen years of teaching, I have seen countless women come to seminary after or in the midst of life-transforming experiences. Some women come to seminary while going through a divorce, and some come to seminary and experience changes in their understandings of their sexuality. Many other women come to seminary in the context of developmental transitions such as children leaving home, graduating from college, or a midlife crisis. Women work at rewriting their lives in theological education. The process of theological education, in some sense, gives many women space and resources for writing their lives in new ways.

Interrelated with narrativity, women and men participate in new forms and shapes of Christian community in theological education. Through worship services, spirituality groups, and feminist classes, students participate in a reality of church that many find full of power and transformation. Following Elisabeth Schüssler Fiorenza, I will call this participation in new forms and shapes of Christianity ekklesiality.

And of course, theology itself is a practice that, one hopes, is inescapable in theological education. As we shall see, the practice of theology within feminist theological education is best described as a *habitus*, one that can be defined as ways of naming God. It is a practical knowledge, but one with particular visions, values, and norms, all aimed at substantive dialogue with the world. Though theological education as a training in *habitus* will emerge throughout this book, special attention will be given to the distinctiveness of the practice of feminist theology as naming God.

2. Shaking the Foundations: The Practice of Narrativity

Who are the subjects of theological education? In many of the theological schools in North America, the subjects of theological education have changed rather dramatically in the last twenty-five years. Once the students in theological education were white, young, and male, largely from working- or middle-class backgrounds. Raised in the church, many aspired to serve God and to become religious professionals. With clear role models before them, these young men were destined to become yet another generation of clerics. Now these subjects are few and far between in many of our schools. Looking at a seminary class (there is no average class today), one sees women in large numbers (often 50 to 80 percent), older students, males and females, African Americans, Hispanic Americans, Native Americans, Asian Americans, and Euro-Americans.[1] Many of these students were not raised in the church; others are lifelong children of the church. Lifestyle differences, theological pluralism, and cultural diversity are apparent if one attends to the subjects of theological education.

Consider just some of the subjects of theological education in a first-year class who enroll in a course titled "Feminist/Womanist Theologies." Julie is a fifty-five-year-old Euro-American widowed grandmother, who is now trying to live productively for the next twenty to thirty years. Ann is a twenty-eight-year-old Euro-American woman with a major in women's studies from an Ivy League school who has been working for the past six years in battered women's shelters and identifies herself as a lesbian Christian. Young is twenty-six, a native of Korea, who finds herself dislocated as a feminist in Korea and as a Korean woman in largely Euro-American feminist classes in the United States. At thirty-three, Michele is a

19

well-known attorney in the city, who, as an African American, is concerned about the leadership crisis in the black church.

Telsa, at twenty-three, is a Euro-American woman from the rural South, deeply committed to ecological issues, who calls herself an evangelical Christian. From the rural Midwest, Jim is a Euro-American male, fifty-two years of age, who introduces himself to the class by identifying himself as a Vietnam veteran and the father of four daughters. May, at thirty-nine years of age, is a Euro-American woman who has had a successful business career but now speaks of feeling burned out and wanting to contribute something to the world. Tina, from Oregon, is forty-two, identifies herself as deeply spiritual and called by God to ministry, but finds the Euro-American mainline denomination she grew up in and seeks ordination in spiritually languishing. Twenty-eight-year-old African American Tom has been a high school math teacher who has loved working with people in his church in Texas since he was an adolescent and who publishes poetry in both religious and secular magazines. As a mother of three and a housewife all her adult life, forty-four-year-old Euro-American Lisa has just experienced the trauma of being left by her husband and seeks transformation from her struggles. Rosanna is a thirty-three-year-old Cuban American from New York City who says she has been pulled into seminary by the tremendous needs of Spanish-speaking immigrants, especially the women.

One of the fundamental questions for the future of theological education is, Who are the subjects of theological education? The question asks us to pay attention, on a quite literal level, to the students. One of the most significant changes in the last twenty years is the presence of women in theological education. It is primarily this change and the nature of this group of theological subjects that I want to explore in this text. By this I don't mean to suggest that women are any one essential or universal subject. Indeed, the needs of women to compose their lives in a variety of different ways against general cultural representations of what it is to be a woman (formed within the intersections of race, class, and sexual orientation) leads to some of the exciting challenges of theological education. As a scholar who specializes in areas of women and religion, and as a woman who has been a student and is now a professor in theological education, I begin here to pose the question, Who are women as subjects of theological education?

This question, I think, cannot be explored simply within the

confines of theological education. The question of women as subjects in theological education, in order to be credible, has to be set in
the context of the present challenges of and for women in society
and in the university. Theological education, long studied in terms
of the internal development of ideas, is shaped by social forces and
by developments of higher education. In order to understand the
challenges and changes in theological education, we must see them
historically, in terms of social conditions, and institutionally, in
terms of institutions with which they react. To pose the question of
women as subjects of theological education, then, we must make
some attempt to understand the changes in roles and work of
women and the accompanying changes in the discursive practices
about women. We must thus understand, given this context, the rise
of women's studies programs and the development of feminist theory as a way to create spaces to explore issues of gender and power
in culture. To ask us to view this question through a broad scope
rather than a narrow lens is exceedingly difficult, but it is the only
way to start charting the challenges women undertake in rewriting
their lives in theological education.

After describing the changes women have experienced in recent
years and the rise of women's studies in the university resulting in
changes in the discursive practices about women, the bulk of this
chapter will explore feminist theology as one space in which women
are writing their lives in feminist practices of theological education,
an activity I will call the practice of narrativity. As a practice, narrativity will require some explaining, precisely because it is used in so
many different ways. For now, by "narrativity" I simply mean the
active agency of writing one's own life: the ongoing construction of
one's own life in the context of human and planetary relations. From
a cultural view I mean to suggest that the dominant stories of what
it is to be a woman have changed and are changing. Narrativity
identifies the felt experience of women as a description of the
process of both their lives and their theological educations. For
women, and perhaps also for men, the need to write new lives is not
a luxury but, as Audre Lorde says of poetry, "a vital necessity of
women's existence."[2] The power to write one's life as an active agent
is the power to participate, potentially and actually, in the determination of cultural and institutional conditions. Narrativity, I will
maintain later, also parallels the praxis of the ecclesiology and the
practical side of theology that are involved in feminist practices of
theological education.

Composing Women's Lives

Mary Catherine Bateson, professor of anthropology and English, speaks of the task that confronts so many women in our culture: the task of composing their lives.[3] This act of creation is different for most of us than for our parents. The traditional narratives, the rules and roles, the pleasures and pains, no longer fit contemporary cultural and political reality. The act of creating oneself in the midst of social and interpersonal relations requires new meanings, symbols, characters, images, and plots. Of course, this act of composing our lives, of finding new spaces of subjectivity, is not universally the same. White middle-class women experience this as composing a life that combines career and home, while for African Americans this choice has defined their lives from the days of slavery on. Toni Morrison observes that this difference lies at the heart of the difference between the writing of white women and black women:

> Black women seem able to combine the nest and the adventure.
> They don't see conflicts in certain areas as do white women.
> They are both safe harbor and ship; they are both inn and trail.[4]

Black feminist Patricia Hill Collins locates the need of black women to define themselves in new ways against what she calls the "seamless web of economy, polity, and ideology."[5]

Yet across race, class, and sexual orientation lines almost everyone today must compose their lives in new ways. The turn to postmodernity signifies in culture that though the established narratives of modernity are not gone, they no longer exist as sure foundations. The persistence of oppression and dehumanization of various social groups and the crisis of global survival suggest that we must write new narratives for flourishing lest we perish by clinging to stories whose realized plots are always destruction.

Such rapid change and continual crisis seems to indicate that not only do we have to compose our lives anew but that the very art of composing, the ongoingness of creation, is itself going to be a central theme in our lives. For many of us in a highly transient society, life transforms itself almost continually. Changing practices of work, of lifestyle, of cultural forms require us to be skilled at living with new beginnings. Stability, assured by traditional bonds of never-changing or slowly changing practices of employment, of family, of community, now appears in our culture as a lost possibility. We must now learn a new art, the art of composing our lives anew and finding in that ongoing act of creation new forms of bonds, community, and identity.

To understand the presence of women in theological schools, we must realize that these women exist within broad cultural changes having to do with employment, reproductive practices, sexual practices and family structures. As Nanette Roberts has observed, "The so-called liberation of women is being articulated and debated by social, political, and religious theorists; its basis lies in the realms of economic and technological change."[6]

White middle-class and working-class women entered the work force in massive numbers during World War II. On the eve of that war, as Carl Degler says, "Over four-fifths of working women were single and only temporarily in the work-force prior to marriage; less than 15 per cent of all married women with husband present were employed, and at that a disproportionate share of the total were black women whose work was not only unskilled and low paid, but was chiefly compelled by low family income."[7] By the 1950s, economic forces in the United States were requiring women to work outside the home in increasing numbers. In 1940, only 15 percent of all married women worked outside the home. By 1960, it was around 30 percent; by 1975, 44 percent of all married women with husband present worked outside the home.[8] Today at least 78 percent of adult women are in the workforce.[9]

Women have always worked, and women's increasing rates of entrance into "public" work display only the gendered identification of work as that which goes on in the public sphere. Many women have worked outside the home. Black women have worked in low-paying jobs, often traveling to other women's homes to work and then returning to their own homes to work some more. Black women's work has not been counted, however, as "work," because of the locus of their work in the private realm (white women's houses). During slavery, 90 to 95 percent of black women worked, and in the years directly after emancipation this percentage moved to roughly 70 percent. In 1880, for instance, roughly 50 percent of black women were in the labor force as compared to about 15 percent of white women. The particularities of black women's work as paid (often domestic) and unpaid (in extended family networks) mean that their work has often been overlooked in dominant modes of social analysis using social class models focusing on social attainment or class conflict.[10]

If women across class lines are now involved in what we call the labor force, they have been largely isolated into low-paying, "feminized" jobs. Eighty percent of women work in the jobs with the lowest 20 percent of pay. Indeed 60 percent of all women are employed in clerical and service sectors, where they toil, as Nancy Fraser has said, as feminized and frequently "sexualized" workers.[11]

The second general cultural change in women's lives has to do with the development of sophisticated reproductive technologies and the emergence and popularity of the birth control pill in the 1960s. Women, and families, could control their reproduction successfully, provided, of course, that they could afford it. At least since the early part of the nineteenth century in the United States, many women indicated a growing desire for birth control, including the practice of abortion.[12] There are at least two implications of the rise of reproductive technologies. First, women could and did limit the number of births, with the fertility rate falling by nearly half between 1960 and 1980.[13] Second, the ability to control the number, let alone the timing of births, along with improved health care for women, resulted in women living longer, having years to fill without mother work. Indeed, if mother work once dominated all the years (and the hours and minutes) of women's lives, by the 1960s mother work lasted only a fourth to a third of women's adult years. And mother work, because of both public schools and changed cultural standards, no longer required as many hours. The model of mother work as definitive of a woman's life appeared, of course, only in recent history and has been class and race specific. The so-called cult of domesticity has never had a great deal of purchase among African American women in the United States, who have traditionally organized communal child care and understood mutual accountability for each other's children.[14]

The third broad cultural trend is changing sexual practices. The sexual revolution had broad effects on American culture, effects largely ignored in the writings on theology and theological education. Sexuality for women is no longer dominated by chastity before marriage and fidelity after marriage, with the average age at which girls become sexually active being sixteen. Marriage no longer defines women's sexuality. Heterosexuality no longer is the only option ever mentioned for women's sexuality and sexual practices. Growing numbers of lesbians and bisexual women not only began to speak out and break the silence, they began to lead theological education and the church into questions about the nature of sexuality.[15] Sexuality became a topic of some choice, with a range of practices understood to be morally, socially, and even (at least for some) religiously acceptable.

The fourth broad cultural trend is changing family practices, and changing perceptions of family. After the 1960s, divorce statistics showed a steady rise, and different family patterns began to be recognized. Again, this change is in part a matter of perception, for the so-called traditional nuclear family is of recent origin, and many groups in the United States have never experienced it as a norm. In addition to changing family patterns, the nuclear family ideology began to shift. The functions assigned to the ideal family since the turn of the nineteenth century—the formation of identity, the nurturing of intimacy, the development of children, and the propagation of morality and values—were narrowed by changing circumstances in economics and social structures and became assumed by other realms or institutions. An important result of this is changing perceptions of approval for working mothers. Another important result is the dramatic rise of single-parent, usually mother-headed, families. It is predicted that in the future at least one-half of all children will live for at least a time in a single-parent family. Since for married, nondivorced women the average age of becoming widowed is fifty-six, most women will be in single family situations for a significant part of their lives. Changing family identity, that is, what constitutes a family, is greatly influenced by new family forms among gays and lesbians as well as new familial practices among single persons.

The changes in work, reproduction, sexuality, and family reveal at least two facts that must be understood in order to grasp the present cultural realities for most women in U.S. culture. First, there are changed realities that are not the result of individual women's choices nor even the result of efforts by a small group of educated intellectuals to interpret feminism. Feminism, more accurately understood, is located within these broader changes that affect the lives of all women (and men). It is important to stress, against any possible misreading, that topics such as family, marriage, and children are still considered extremely important by many women. But not by all women. And those women who find marriage, family, and children important will have to define them in new ways, both because of the necessity of combining work and family and because of the choices now offered them by changing technological and social factors.

The second changed fact is equally important. For there is now the recognition that the normative homogeneous values have themselves been an ideology to cover and silence a diversity of practices, narratives, and roles for women in U.S. culture. Women have never all fit the dominant narrative. Within this dialectical space—that the normative narrative does not work for even the middle class, and that women who have lived alternative patterns now find space to express their narratives—women, seen as a marker of plurality and difference, are struggling, coping, experimenting with new ways to live. And with these changes in the culture, changes that most of us know and are affected by, arise new theories of explanation, critique, and change centered in women's studies in American universities.

Women's Studies
and the University

With the changing realities and ideologies of women came dramatic changes in the discursive practices about women. By discursive practice I mean the way theorists write, talk, and act in relation to a particular subject matter. Indeed, so dramatic were the changes in understandings of "woman" and about women, a new field called "women's studies" soon arose in the academy. This field of study drew on a variety of disciplines to consider a range of questions and issues about women in areas such as the representation of women in literature, the specificity of women's writing, the role of women in various historical eras, and the presence of women in the professions, both in terms of how women succeed in the professions and how the professions, such as law, treat women. Women's studies and feminist theory developed as women, and sometimes men, began to analyze the complex identities, roles, and practices of women and men. The analysis of the historical construction of women, and of men, took place in many of the disciplines represented in the contemporary academy.

Women's studies is a distinct way of organizing knowledge in the academy. It is multidisciplinary, attempting to look within and across the disciplines at the organization of political, cultural, and personal life in regard to gender. I want to use the term *feminist theory* for the approaches used in women's studies, though I recognize that this term is itself controversial. The controversy arises out of both the effectiveness of feminist theory (is it too tied to the problems it seeks to escape?) and the media representation of feminism (is it too tied to radical caricature to even gain entrance into public debate?). Yet, the term *feminism* deserves to be respected historically for constructing new discourses of women's lives and for using gender as a way to analyze cultural politics.

There are a variety of feminist approaches, many relating to theoretical perspectives popular in the academy.[16] Liberal feminism uses arguments for equal rights to correct inequalities concerning women. Radical feminism envisions a new social order based on woman's unique or distinct qualities. Socialist feminists understand gender as interconnected to race and class and analyze women through a social perspective. Poststructuralist feminists are interested in the depth orders of gender that run through language, politics, and subjectivity.

In the midst of its own variety of perspectives, feminist theory's particular contribution is its investigation into gender as a form of social-personal construction and distribution of power. Gender studies arose in feminist theory, according to Joan Scott, as a way of getting at "the fundamentally social quality of distinctions based on sex."[17] Gender studies have been applied to good effect in textual studies, in history, in cultural studies, and, of course, in economics. Indeed, gender studies have become not simply an analysis of how society sees men and women as different and makes them so, but how different categories and structures are marked and constituted through a patriarchal ordering of gender division. As Scott maintains, gender is both a "constitutive element in social relations based on perceived differences between the sexes and gender is a primary way of signifying relationships of power."[18]

Concerned with how social arrangements get established through sexual difference, the study of gender includes at least four elements. First, gender arrangements become established through cultural symbols, and the meanings they invoke. The Marlboro man as a cultural image for Euro-American men and the Barbie doll as a cultural image for Euro-American women are symbols representing the importance of images. The second element of the study of gender attends to normative concepts that set forth the interpretive horizons of the symbol. The Marlboro man is a popular cultural image that mirrors various philosophical, psychological, and religious theories of the Euro-American man as autonomous, rational, strong, and ready to conquer the wild. The Barbie doll image mirrors concepts of the Euro-American woman found in those same theories as pretty and a perfect mannequin for various costumes and adornments. Interestingly, as white middle-class women have gone to work in large numbers, Barbie has simply added a briefcase and work clothes as one of her many costumes. And as multiculturalism comes to the foreground in cultural representation, the category of Barbie is broadened to include an African American doll and various "ethnic" dolls.

Analysis of political and social institutions, of how they relate to and reinforce or disrupt the concepts and myths, composes the third element of the study of gender. The church, as an institution, has long promulgated ideologies of the superiority of men and inferiority of women in its social organization as well as in its myths and theories. The refusal to allow women to occupy positions of religious leadership outside of women's organizations reinforced patriarchal myths and concepts. Paradoxically, however, the training that women received in those women's organizations in the late nineteenth century may well have contributed to women's move into the public realm, arguing new concepts and offering new images.

The fourth element of the study of gender is the interpretation of subjective identity, how personal experience is constructed in relation to the other three elements. Modern culture represents women as taking pleasure in their lower status and dependency, and men as always being in control and avoiding feelings as much as possible. These representations of individual experiencing, at least in part, are always linked to the images, concepts, and institutions of culture.

Gender studies, as Scott maintains, include the exploration of what such gender arrangements have to do with arrangements of power. As Scott maintains, "Established as an objective set of references, concepts of gender structure perception and the concrete and symbolic organization of all social life. To the extent that these references establish distributions of power (differential control over or access to material and symbolic resources), gender becomes implicated in the conception and construction of power itself."[19] The distribution of power in Christianity is a good example. Despite all the religious claims to equality symbolized and conceptualized in baptism, where all receive equally the benefits of Christ, the distribution of power in terms of access to the manufacturing of symbols, to the articulation of concepts, and to the management of institutions has favored men over women. In addition, the narratives of men and women in Christianity have often been different, with the use of the doctrine of creation to assert equal roles in principle but different in practice for men and women.

The very existence of women's studies signifies the changing realities of women's lives and has contributed significantly to understanding how social institutions and structures have been organized through gender divisions. Feminist theory, especially in those forms influenced by poststructuralism, also considers how society itself becomes gendered, that is, how social institutions and structures get assigned feminine and masculine attributes with their relative valuational status. For instance, in modernity the public realm has been valued as masculine and elevated to the highest good. Meanwhile the private realm is seen as the feminine, literally the feminine sphere, and is disvalued as secondary and dependent. In relation to theology and theological education, a quite pertinent example is the genderfication—the construction through gender identification—of knowledge and religion. Knowledge is located in the masculine realm, the public, and seen as objective, universal, autonomous.[20] Religion, on the other hand, is the opposite, or "other" than knowledge, located in the private realm. It is defined through an understanding of the affections as irrational, sentimental, impulsive. Religion is thus separated from knowledge, and reason is removed from the affections, as women are separated from men in the gender definitions of modernity. Religion, like the gender construct of women, serves the needs of private individuals that arise at the limits of the public: birth, death, suffering, linkages to nature and transcendence, aesthetic values, carrying on traditions. All such needs are seen as unnecessary and thus reside in the private realm, ordered and controlled with no claims to public knowledge. As a number of feminist critics have pointed out, this division of masculine and feminine constitutes a particular view of the unencumbered self and universal reason that requires the normativity of "objective" knowledge and strict adherence to the privacy of religious belief.[21]

Women's studies, and with it feminist theories, represent the dramatic shift in the discursive practices of and about women. New topics, new approaches, new understandings have all been arrived at through feminist theories. Such theories have changed traditional fields such as history, literature, and sociology. And for feminist practices of theology and theological education, the impact of women's studies and feminist theories provides innumerable possibilities.

Narratives and the Subjects
of Theological Education

Thus the students whom we welcomed at the beginning of this chapter both represent and constitute all these changes and possibilities. Within the limits the women and men may have personally, culturally, and structurally, they must choose to write their lives in some way. The changes in work, family, reproduction, and sexuality, along with the new resources of women's studies, are not due to intents of individual students. The students themselves are, in some way, created by these cultural and intellectual forces, not vice versa. But on a deeply existential level, in the reality of the day to day, each woman and man has the possibility and responsibility to compose her or his life. The women, and the men, cannot or do not have to fit in predetermined narratives or cultural myths. The present situation of cultural, and certainly of theological education, forces a crisis, and thus a possibility, of narrativity for nearly everyone in our midst.

Take Julie, whom we met at the beginning of this chapter. Julie is fifty-five, a widow and a grandmother, who now finds herself largely alone, her partner gone and her children living across the globe. Julie assumed that, like June Cleaver in the "Leave It to Beaver" television series, she would live in a close, extended-family network in her hometown until she died. Now, she must construct, quite literally, a new life for herself. She really doesn't have a model from her past, though she has bits and pieces of stories of women and men she has known, but nothing that can be readily adapted to her present reality. Fascinated by feminist literary theory, which explores how and what women have written, Julie resonates with Patricia Yeager's notion of the honey-mad woman who has a variety of relationships to language, and Julie adds, to God.[22] She wants to explore how women have used language itself to create their lives and how words can create new stories for women to live. How will she live this part of her Christian journey?

Michele, the thirty-three-year-old African American lawyer, has resources far beyond what she thought she'd ever have, and thus for her, far greater responsibilities to love God and others. She is deeply inspired by Delores Williams in *Sisters in the Wilderness*, who writes against the images and out of the struggles of black women as surrogate mothers in this culture, and by Toni Morrison, Gloria Naylor, Audre Lorde, and Alice Walker, who write narratives of and for black women. Understanding that the oppression African American women face has to do with interlocking structures of racism, sexism, and classism, Michele wants to use her legal training and her theological education to provide new opportunities for self-understanding and self-achievement for African American women in this culture. Through providing leadership within the black church, Michele wants to be involved in the political struggles of African American women in her city. In this way, Michele also wants to model a new narrative of Christian life for black women, but she understands that providing ministerial leadership is but one form of a long tradition of African American women's participation in the religious and political movements of her city.

Jim, perhaps of all the students, seems set in the typical Euro-American male pattern, living out a narrative for white men that spans the years of this century. But he studies feminist theology because he is worried about his daughters and wants to help them learn to protect themselves, rather than assuming a man will always be there to protect them. In the class, listening to all the stories women students tell about harassment and physical violence, he becomes riveted with the reading of Susan Faludi's *Backlash: The Undeclared War against American Women*.[23] By midsemester Jim is talking about redefining his identity as a Euro-American male minister as one who needs to help persons address the existential, cultural, and political crises of contemporary life.

These students, and the many others I have interviewed and taught, are actively engaged in the practice of composing their lives in and through theological education. This practice of composing we might call narrativity, for the term reminds us not only of the existential and political fact that women write new lives because they must, but also of the history of women writing, the practicality of narrative itself, and the way narrativity laces across Christian histories and journeys. The notion of narrativity as a fundamental practice of feminist theological education allows us a multiperspectival way to understand how women and men intentionally create their lives in relation to their culture, their bodies, their individual experiences, and their Christian communities.

When women began to write in significant numbers, they wrote narratives, both fiction and autobiography. Sidonie Smith cites many causes for the turn especially to autobiography in the eighteenth and nineteenth centuries: the stress on the self made in different ways by the Industrial Revolution, Freudianism, Victorianism, Social Darwinism, the movements of democratization, the increased ability of autobiographies to reach a reading public, and the call for history to be written based on autobiography.[24] In a variety of ways, modernity creates a reflective subject. Though men have openness and adventure in their modern narratives, women, serving as the "other" of men, are too often defined, as Carolyn Heilbrun suggests, through closure and passivity if they are white.[25] African American women, as Patricia Hill Collins suggests, get defined through images of mammy, matriarch, welfare mother, or Jezebel.[26]

Or do they? Some feminist theorists maintain that the very act of writing by women was already an act of subversion, resistance, and emancipation. Patricia Yeager maintains that women writers seized words and used them for their own purposes, redefining their own position and identity.[27] Claudia Tate argues that in writing, black women have learned to exceed their boundaries.[28]

If there is then truth in Virginia Woolf's notion that history underwent radical transformation from the time that women first began to write, part of that truth is that in many different ways women took on an active authorial agency that in turn created different lives, different relationships, and a different world. Feminist theories, then, offer to us the reality that to write, and by extension to live one's life as the act of writing, is to be able to resist oppression and definition by the others. The narrativity of one's life, in a sense, is one possibility of emancipation: to free one's self from definition imposed on one and to live one's life in the activity of writing. Here fiction imitates life, but also the reverse is true: writing, be it literal or lived, is an act of creating one's life in new ways.

The use of the concepts of "narrative" and "narrativity" is also employed in philosophy to name the practice of lived experience. Alasdair MacIntyre in *After Virtue* contends that narrative history is the most essential genre of describing human activity.[29] Personal identity is not fixed, according to MacIntyre, but is constructed through narrative, or, in his language, narrative and identity presuppose each other. David Carr argues that narrative pushes beyond actual texts and acts of writing to name historical experience of time; for example, humans experience the passing of time in a narrative way.[30] Narrative as an apt description for human experience brings together what modern theories tended to divide: event and meaning, action and intention.[31] The meanings of our actions are "explained" in our stories as we construct our agency. Our stories are related to but not determined by factors such as events beyond which we have no control, other actors to whom we are in relation, and traditions that we appropriate or resist.

The concept of narrativity allows us to bring diachronic elements, or historical developments of past events and processes, together with synchronic elements, or contemporary structures and dynamics. It portrays, as MacIntyre suggests, that we are never authors of our narratives, but only coauthors, since there are always other influences that can be neither ignored nor minimized. Narrativity allows the most credible description of the "I" of identity—an ongoing process shaped by and shaping other agents, traditions, and institutions. In words sympathetic to our notion of narrativity as a practice, David Carr notes that "narrative structure has a pre-eminently practical character."[32]

Perhaps it is because narrativity has a practical character that the term has a long resonance within the history of Christian practices. As I have already suggested, theology, at least since Augustine, has been attuned to narrative as a kind of Christian activity. The Christian belief in baptism and the resultant responsibility that one has to live in grace is envisioned as a type of narrativity. From the medieval confessional to the pietist class meeting, the reflective awareness and narrative direction of the believer's life is emphasized.

Our story is written, at least in part, in the context of "sacred" stories, to use the language of Stephen Crites.[33] In recent years the notion of narrative in Christianity has been primarily applied to the sacred scriptures themselves. Hans Frei, for instance, insists that Christians live within the story.[34] In a quite different way, David Tracy suggests that Christian theology is a reading of scripture as religious classics.[35]

A complaint against narrative as a Christian practice might be that narrative as a metaphor tends to promote a certain closure: a beginning, a middle, and an end. Certainly the closure of women's lives in Christianity has been invoked by the use of narratives, as when it is suggested we fit our lives into the biblical stories. Christian narratives, at least as they have been told, tend to silence women's own words about themselves as a way to control women's sexuality. Sidonie Smith has suggested, for example, that Renaissance Christianity allowed four scripts to women: that of the nun, the queen, the wife, and the mother. Smith observes, "These four life scripts establish certain relationships among female speech, female sexuality, and female goodness, among the closed mouth, the closed womb, and enclosure in house or convent."[36] But women today turn this closure of narrativity inside out, suggesting that narrativity as a description of our lives and to which we are called in Christian witness is the ongoing process of actively rewriting our lives.

Christianity is, among other things, a kind of "in-process" narrativity of God and world. The way the Christian story is told at any given time and place is conditioned by the historical location of the tellers. The rural Christian woman in Kansas one hundred years ago lived one narrative while women living at present in Atlanta compose different ones. Narratives, after all, can be expressed through many different plots and styles. And Christianity is itself a living tradition whose theological symbols point to the openness of its narrativity.[37]

Thus, the practice of narrativity allows for a certain kind of in-terrelationship or texture among the traditions, communities, and institutions to which we belong and which belong to us. And yet, there is also a subjectivity involved, some kind of deliberate agency that enables one to make choices, to opt for certain plots and not for others, to pursue development of virtues. In other words, narrativ-ity is neither pure social determination nor autonomous individual-ism, but rather a way to name the practical reality of what we have to face: the ongoing activity of writing our lives.[38] To a certain extent this is merely a Christian anthropological statement: like Augustine in his *Confessions*, we have to interpret our past in the process of moving forward. But it is intensified in particular ways due to the days in which we live, days in which among other things the pres-ence of women has changed, quite literally, the student bodies in theological education. No metaphor for the agency of what students do in theological education, let alone in life, will be perfect. Cer-tainly the physical experiences of the body and the social experi-ences of institutions will always limit the metaphor of narrativity by reminding us of concrete physical and social realities that, while they have to be expressed in words, always exist in excess of all dis-courses and words.

Despite its limits, narrativity gives us a kind of multiperspectival way to speak about the agency of subjects in theological education. Education, whatever its form and understanding, presupposes some process of forming, constructing, or developing human subjects. Christian theology has often involved some intentional awareness about narrativity as a theme of Christianity. Narrativity is a practice that allows us to consider the intersection of education, theology, and the agency of women in constructing their lives; it thus opens up for us one way of understanding the impact of the presence of women in theological education.

Practicing Narrative Agency

Feminist practices of theological education create narrative agency in the dual sense of providing space for the development of agency and by composing particular narratives for personal and so-cial flourishing. Indeed, in my experience women create through feminist practices of theological education a new experience of sub-jectivity. Women and men write new narratives for their lives and in this process create new forms of narrative agency.

I want, therefore, to consider some of the ways in which feminist theology enables this agency. Practices of feminist agency, like all other visions of agency, will use base points to map out or define the nature of agency. The conceptual status of a base point is that of a heuristic device rather than an eternal norm or a universal category. There are four base points around which feminist narrative agency tends to revolve: the naming of women's experience; the explication of differences (a principle of contextuality versus essentialism); the emphasis of actively reconstructing and "using" traditions; and a set of shared moral values constructing, among other things, types of moral agency.

Base Point 1: The Voicing of Women's Experiences

In a way, the simple naming of the experiences of women by women has been the first step toward creating a narrative agency of and by women. Feminist theology, at least in the latter half of the twentieth century, can be said to begin officially with the 1960 publication of Valerie Saiving's article "The Human Situation: A Feminine View," in which she criticized Reinhold Niebuhr and Anders Nygren for identifying sin universally with self-assertion and love with selflessness, arguing that such forms of sin were based not on human experience but on man's experience.[39] In the space cleared by her criticism, Saiving probed the nature of woman's experience as different from man's and the need for theology to reflect upon the experience of woman. Rosemary Radford Ruether, the first feminist theologian to produce a systematic theology based on women's experiences, lists the dimensions of women's experiences as the bodily experience of women, the devaluation of the body by patriarchy, the negation and trivialization of women in patriarchy, and also the grace-filled experiences of women affirming themselves.[40] Nelle Morton realized that in the very speaking and hearing of women's experiences, women are, in her wonderful phrase, "hearing one another to speech."[41]

Though feminists no longer assume there is a woman's experience (which we will discuss under our second base point), the notion that women name their experiences and identify experiences as loci of theological practice is an extremely important step in creating narrative agency. The naming of experience is the activity of constructing an agent who is responsible for her reflection, her practice, her spirituality.[42] One of the most consistent parallels in the stories women told me was the importance of learning to name their experiences within feminist classes, spirituality groups, and worship services. Many women spoke of how often their experiences had been dismissed, ignored, belittled, or just never mentioned within the "traditional" classrooms of theological education.

Narrative agency is created and used as women begin to name their experiences. Women often speak of experiences not often considered in theology: experiences of mothering, of rape, of women's sexualities, of being daughters, of female friendships, of survival, of religion in the midst of domestic work of home, of church, of local community. Women thus name experiences and in so doing begin to narrate the meaning of these experiences in new ways. This surfacing of experiences and the speaking of experiences in new ways is one of the reasons that women and men use poetry and novels a great deal in feminist theology.

Base Point 2: The Privileging of Contextuality and Difference over Universalism and Essentialism

Feminist theologians also faced a problem with the term *experience:* are all women's experiences the same? Feminist theology as reflecting the experiences of white, middle-class women was called to question by the "experiences" of African American women, of lesbians, of Hispanic American women, and of Asian American women. Jacqueline Grant, in *White Women's Christ and Black Women's Jesus,* examines various white women's Christologies, showing that despite the differences between biblical, liberationist, and radical feminist Christologies, all share a common assumption of white women's experiences of Christ.[43] Grant then begins to explore the experiences of Jesus in black women's experience and in womanist thought. The works of Carter Heyward and Mary Hunt explore the distinctive experiences of lesbians, revealing the heterosexism of much of feminist theology, and use the experience of lesbian relationships to create new theological symbols and metaphors. Chung Hyun Kyung names the experiences of Korean women and narrates their meaning within the theological symbols of Christology, Mariology, and spirituality.[44]

The narrative agency of feminist theology cannot be that of a universal abstraction of white, middle-class experience. Ada María Isasi-Díaz argues that adding Hispanic women to feminism is not like baking a cake, not just one more ingredient to add. Rather, white feminists must learn about Hispanic culture and learn to define experience in light of relation to Hispanic culture and thus "to assume responsibility for the systematic analysis of ethical prejudice and racism."[45] The plurality of voices represented in feminist theologies results in a privileging of difference in theoretical and political constructs.

The insistence on differences requires a recognition of complexity in relation to experience of oppression. The differences among black, mujerista, and white women are not simply additions to the oppression suffered by white women. That is, women are not oppressed fundamentally as women, and then oppressed additionally because of race and class. Rather, oppression is interlocking or multiplicative. As Janet Jakobsen observes, the ideology of gender gets interstructured with ideologies of class and race.[46]

This is not to discard "woman" as a category completely, but it is to render it problematic as a clear and precise category. Theoretically the problem of the meaning and use of the category "woman" became known as the "essentialist" debates, the debates over whether there was such a thing as *woman*, or whether that category itself already contained the problems of patriarchy. In feminist theory, Elizabeth Spelman's provocative book *Inessential Woman* displays how the assumption of white, middle-class, heterosexual women's experience in feminist theory has consistently hidden and ignored the naming, let alone privileging, of differences among women.[47]

This base point locates a narrative agency in terms of allowing a certain positionality of women, in the sense that in the critique of patriarchy, "woman" becomes first a general category within which all differences are denied. But positionality also becomes a kind of positive attribute of narrative agency as feminists speak of identity and agency as always in flux, always in relative position to the changing historical context.[48]

The understanding of contextuality as positionality includes two points. First, as already stated, the concept of woman is a relational term identifiable only within a constantly changing context. Second, the position that women find themselves in can be actively utilized (rather than transcended) as a location for the construction of meaning, a place from where meaning is constructed rather than simply a place where meaning can be *discovered* (the meaning of "femaleness").

Base Point 3: The Agency of Reconstruction

The preferred term for understanding what it is that feminist theologians do in relation to scriptures and the symbol system is the *reconstruction of tradition.* Feminists understand that they must actively
redo the meaning of symbols and the use of tradition, away from patriarchal constructs and toward ongoing transformation and flourishing. This aspect of reconstruction is itself a basic practice of the
ongoing nature of Christian traditions: different historical periods
have used scriptures in different ways, emphasized different parts of
scripture, and always reconstructed tradition in light of the needs
of the day. This type of agency has generally been the "responsibility"
of particular men. That is to say, officially speaking, certain groups of
men have been assigned the task of narrative agency. In feminist
practices of theological education, women participate in the ongoing
reconstruction of a Christian symbol system. There are at least two
aspects of this base point that enable narrative agency. The first is the
tremendous work done by feminist theologians in the interpretations
of traditions. The second is the claiming of women's activity as the
locus and site of Christian reflection on God.

One woman, now a graduate of theological education and a university chaplain, wrote of women's quest for tradition:

> When I teach classes about the body practices of Medieval
> women, I have learned that many women come to hear how
> ancient and now accepted women of Christian faith came to
> themselves and their ministries. The women want me to tell
> them more of the stories—as if we were around a campfire at
> Girl Scouts, or like we were told other noninclusive Bible sto-
> ries when we were children—very few of them about women.
> They come to classes to hear these stories—those talks of
> women who have always found sacred spaces with unexpected
> possibilities for transformation and justice. They want to know
> as many details as possible. They want the information. It is not
> only for modelling of metaphor. They want the data—the story
> line, because they want to go and tell it. Because they sus-
> pected, perhaps, that these stories were there but they demand
> more than reference to them. Vagaries are inadequate. They
> want details and they want to try to tell you the story back
> double-checking, so that they can tell it properly.[49]

As an example of the work feminist theologians have done in
reading the tradition, consider the tremendous amount of work

done on just the scriptures. Feminist theologians have paid a great deal of attention to what the scriptures say about women and how the scriptures have been used against women. The lens of feminist theology and the power of women's faith experiences have provoked the careful focusing of patriarchal translations, as when Phoebe's title *diakonis* is translated "deaconess" or "servant" when it is applied to her and "minister" or "deacon" when it is used to describe a male leader. Likewise feminist theology examines patriarchal interpretations (as when Eve is simply blamed for sin rather than noted for enabling Adam, the generic human, to become a particular man) and patriarchal oversights (as when the Samaritan woman in John 4 is not the focus of the call to mission, or when the rape of a woman in Judges 19 is ignored or belittled in commentaries).

Feminist theological work on the Bible also concentrates on forgotten or largely ignored women of the scriptures, such as Hagar, Shiphrah, Nympha of Laodicea, and Prisca. Feminist scholars of scripture and other Christian traditions have noted both how frequently the presence of women is overlooked and how rarely women's lives have actually been recorded and named.

In addition, feminist theological scholarship has to do with the authority of the Bible, how it comes to be used against women as a tool of oppression and how it might be used as support for emancipation. Elisabeth Schüssler Fiorenza suggests that the Bible should be understood as "prototype," engendering possibilities of creative transformation, rather than as archetype, containing eternal or ontological truths that apply to any and all situations.[50] Such a turn to reading the Bible as prototype allows us to appreciate how the Bible itself was formed in practical situations in the church and how it models for us some ways the early Christians attempted to live their faith out in the church and culture.

The second aspect of narrative agency involves claiming women's reconstructive activity as the locus and site of Christian reflection on God. Narrative agency is created by women using the Bible, retrieving forgotten stories, actively engaging the systematic distortion in interpretation and exegesis, and resisting patriarchal stories within the scripture itself. The Bible is neither a story that we fit our lives into (denying the historical contextuality of the Bible and the narrative differences within scripture itself) nor a text that we interpret until it reflects a deep existential experience. It is neither rule book nor mirror, but rather material within which the narrative agency of women constructs the ongoing living narratives and symbols of Christianity. Theology is about the interpretation of texts, but an interpretation in which the meaning of texts includes an emphasis upon their effectiveness, their use for emancipation and transformation.

One way of distinguishing the human being is that of the symbol user who, through language and other modes of expression, has the ability to create worlds. In Christianity, women have been denied this power, at least in terms of the production of religious symbols and practices. That women use feminist theologies to take upon themselves the agency of reconstructing symbols of church, God, sin, and so on will be apparent as this book unfolds. In such reconstruction, women assume the responsibility for critically evaluating and creating the ongoing life of Christian symbols and narratives. As I have suggested elsewhere, such reconstruction is nothing less than the startling claim that feminist theology is, at least from one view, a proclamation of the Word, that feminist words today carry the weight of God's word.[51]

Base Point 4: The Creation of Moral Agency and Feminist Virtues

The fourth base point continues the stress on reconstruction, responsibility, and agency through the ongoing creation of moral agency. The area of feminist ethics includes often-overlooked topics of ethics, identifies specific moral virtues, and creates moral agency. Central to almost all feminist theology is a concern for ethics, since the substantive content of feminist theology has to do with oppression and justice. Indeed, feminist theology is in a sense closer to many of the various historic traditions of Christian theology than is most modern theology in that ethics are an essential part, not a secondary discipline, of theological formation.

As we shall see in the next chapter, ethical concerns become a primary ecclesial definition and concern, forming feminist theology, like other forms of liberation theologies, into a mystical-political theology. Feminist theologians have drawn attention to specific ethical concerns of violence against women, ecology, sexuality, racism, classism, anti-Semitism, and abortion. Certainly within contemporary theology, many feminist theologians are the ones calling attention to the injustices of heterosexism and to the theological considerations of the nature of sexuality. Likewise, feminist theologians and ethicists have addressed environmental destruction by demonstrating how the same type of binary logic used against women is employed against the earth. Raising the cultural consciousness about violence against women has been primarily the work of feminist theologians, activists, and theorists.

Within this work of feminist ethics, which treats specific topics as well as ethical theory, feminist ethics has also created certain types of virtues of moral agency. Virtues are, to quote Alasdair MacIntyre, "an acquired human quality the possession and exercise of which tends to enable us to achieve those goods which are internal to practices and the lack of which effectively prevents us from achieving any such goods."[52] Virtues are the forms and qualities of human agency that allow us to address ethical topics, to be moral persons. Virtues name that aspect of being human that allows us to be moral agents in the world. There are many ways feminist practices of theological education constitute virtues such as reading and writing, social activism and witness, liturgies of healing that oppose injustice, and justice-based spirituality groups. And, as in any movement, conflict and debate continually occur about the key virtues.

Katie Cannon, in *Black Womanist Ethics*, uses the writings of black women, especially of Zora Neale Hurston, to inscribe the virtues of invisible dignity, quiet grace, and unshouted courage.[53] Cannon examines how these virtues have allowed women to survive with moral integrity against all odds. Cannon tells us that her approach is not an attempt to prescribe a universal ethic:

> My goal is not to arrive at my own prescriptive or normative ethic. Rather, what I am pursuing is an investigation (a) that will help Black women, and others who care, to understand and to appreciate the richness of their own moral struggle through the life of the common people and the oral tradition; (b) to further understandings of some of the differences between ethics of life under oppression and established moral approaches which take for granted freedom and a wide range of choices.[54]

Cannon provides one view of the moral agency of black women operating under conditions of domination and the struggle for survival rather than, as for many white women, economic success and the quest for self-expression.

Beverly Harrison has suggested that the basic virtues of feminist ethics are the activity of love, embodiment, and connectedness. Love, Harrison maintains, is the power to "act-each-other-into-well-being."[55] Harrison argues that women must recall the power of nurturing, the power of the human activity of love. Since moral theology has been dominated by an active body/mind dualism, feminists must also construct embodiment as a moral value. For Harrison, this virtue is connected to recognizing that all of our knowledge is body-mediated knowledge and thus we must learn that our feelings, such as anger, are also part of the way we know. Finally, the virtue of mutuality has to do with a quality of friendship reciprocity among self, others, and world. The elaboration of moral virtues, in various forms, is extremely important in feminist narrativity. In literature and philosophy, in theology, and in religious writings, women are rarely seen as moral agents in terms of political-cultural relations. At most, they are seen as moral in a private domestic fashion, where morality is reduced to private habits of drinking, smoking, and sex. To make women moral agents as representative of moral agency is, as Ruth Smith has suggested, a central moral task: "Becoming the subject of one's own actions is a social and historical process key to liberation politically, socially, and psychologically so that we no longer collude in our own oppression and so that we can attempt to change conditions of life negation and alienation into conditions of affirmation and fulfillment."[56]

Conclusion

That feminist practices of theological education include narrativity is not surprising. Education has often been discussed in terms of the formation of the individual, as in the notion of a liberal arts education that cultivates the individual for a well-balanced life. Almost every view of education includes some notion of the formation of the self. Greek *paideia* sought to cultivate in a subject the wisdom and virtues necessary for the polis. Modern educational structures seek to form the subject into an autonomous subject who can make universal, objective judgments. Professional education seeks to provide professional skills, forming the student into an expert who solves problems. Each of these views gives rise to particular educational structures, curricular emphases, and even physical arrangements of space and time.

Education, we might say, involves the space of forming or constructing subjectivity. The poignancy of feminist theological education is, on the one hand, the necessity for constructing new forms of narrativity and, on the other hand, the lack of models, forms, and shapes for these to take. This is why, whether or not women explicitly identify with feminist practices of theological education, they are in some sense touched by them. Women today, in theological education as in Christianity and in the broader culture, are engaged in the narrativity of composing their lives.

So narrativity is an old practice, but one, we might say, becoming radically transformed. Maxine Greene, in *Dialectic of Freedom*, writes of the need to create ourselves in education in the midst of the complexities of the present social-cultural realities:

> It seems evident that all this holds relevance for a conception of education—if education is conceived as a process of futuring, of releasing persons to become different, of provoking persons to repair lacks and to take action to create themselves. Action signifies beginnings or the taking of initiative; and, in education, beginnings must be thought possible if authentic learning is to occur.[57]

The feminist practice of narrativity in theological education provokes persons to create themselves. To accomplish this provocative work, certain themes of education that run through this chapter need now to be made explicit.

Three themes seem necessary to nurture education as a space for narrativity: imagination, justice, and dialogue. By educational themes, I mean those values that are also conditions under which learning occurs. They are involved in the creation of physical spaces, in the way we relate to one another, in how we choose what is studied, and what is read. Education depends upon particular values and conditions. Certain themes must be privileged, while others must be neglected, marginalized, or opposed. In the final chapter of this book we shall contemplate at least a partial vision of a feminist educational process, but for now we need only to render explicit certain themes of an educational process already involved in the feminist practice of narrativity.

The theme of imagination includes the conditions of possibility for subjects to place themselves in new roles, stories, and patterns. The development of the imagination is necessary if subjects are to write their lives in new ways. As I have suggested, the use of poetry and prose in feminism relates to the need and ability to envision life, be it personal, interpersonal, or social, in new ways. Imagination involves practices of reading, as persons learn the ways of imaginative construction in various texts and as they approach texts through critical thinking. Imagination is the ability to think differently about the past, the present, and the future.

The theme of dialogue names the conditions of possibility to listen and to speak, to hear and to be heard. Dialogue, as we shall see in chapter 5, involves not endless talk but encounter and change. Dialogic relationships can influence the ways in which the educational process is constructed and experienced. As Edward Farley has pointed out, "hermeneutics," or interpretation, cuts across both texts and situations.[58] To name the interpretation as itself dialogical means to be open to hearing different ways and to be open to hearing critique of one's own position. Imagination and dialogue are needed together in feminist practices of narrativity, for dialogue gives resources to the imagination and grounds the envisionment in the context of real lives, while the imagination allows the dialogue to apply to one's life.

Justice, for many readers, may well be the most controversial of the three themes. Justice, as we shall see in chapter 3, involves deliberation, representation, and construction within community. Justice means that everyone gets a voice in self-determination, and that everyone is allowed and encouraged to have the resources necessary to write his or her life. Concerned not merely with the distribution of goods, justice also entails an examination of the very nature and process of life together. As Iris Marion Young observes, justice is coextensive with the political. As an educational process, justice includes how and what we read as well as how we live together. Without rendering this theme explicit, we may fail to see that the act of women composing their lives is, at its deepest level, both a personal and social quest for justice. Justice allows the ethical to constitute the dialogical and the imaginative, while the imaginative and the dialogic combine to provide justice with new visions of flourishing.

3. Places of Grace:
The Practice of Ekklesia

In chapter 2 we examined how women engage in the practice of narrativity in feminist liberation Christianity. In this chapter the focus within feminist liberation Christianity shifts to a related practice: that of both naming and creating the ekklesia, with its attendant discursive construction of ecclesiology.[1] Writers of books on theological education have pointed to the importance of church for theological education. Joseph Hough and John Cobb argue in *Christian Identity and Theological Education* that understanding the identity of Christianity is the central problem for theological education.[2] David Kelsey, in his *To Understand God Truly*, stresses the importance of understanding the church to interpret theological education.[3] And H. Richard Niebuhr in *The Purpose of the Church and Its Ministry* declares that a clear understanding of church is central to interpreting theological education. "Much confusion and uncertainty in theological schools today seems to be due to lack of clarity about the community—the Church; about its form and matter, its relations and compositions."[4]

In most writings on theological education, the "church" that is referred to is the mainline modern Protestant/Catholic church. In recent years this church has faced the loss of many members, cries against its spiritual declines, internal critiques of its theological and practical individualism, and challenges to its missions of charity rather than justice. Many theologians are critical of the individualism, privatism and blandness of the "church." Peter Hodgson has suggested that the church has become perverted through privatism and individualism: "Frequently the churches have functioned as nothing more than means of satisfying private therapeutic needs through counseling, ideology, and clublike activities."[5] Jürgen Moltmann and many influenced by him have also raised the criticism of how the church has functioned as a kind of cult of the private individual, or, as Johannes Baptist Metz has called it, bourgeois

45

religion.[6] Theologians join clergy and laypersons in a common critique of the church and Christian religion.

Women in the church and in theology also participate in this critique and challenge. Women challenge the church as to whether or not it really is true to the Christian message and credible to contemporary human existence. Does the church offer an adequate spirituality to connect with each other, with God, with the earth? Are the forms of community, growing out of the nineteenth century, really adequate to a multicultural, highly transient, urban society? Is the purpose of the church to be a place to strengthen individual piety or is it to denounce sin and announce grace?

In my experience women with criticisms of the church, much more often than men, are told to love it or leave it. But women, in the church and in theological education, have not so much left the church and formed new denominations as they have called for the transformation of present ecclesial reality. As I will contend throughout this chapter, the distinctiveness of feminist liberationist Christianity is both its critique of present ecclesial reality and its anticipation of what the church can mean, can be, and must become. If one looks at women actively engaging in feminist practices of theological education, what I think one sees is the emancipatory transformation of the church, the emancipation of the church from its own patriarchal and dehumanizing practices, and the transformation of the church into a new nature and mission as ekklesia. The ekklesia names the material corporate existence that is today one expression of Christian dreams and desires, the anticipation of the new out of the unrealized possibilities of the present.

Our first task is to see this emergent church in our midst, to hear what is to be heard, and to experience the reality, including the struggles and questions, of ekklesia within feminist practices of theological education. Only after we stand in these spaces of grace, often called women-church in feminist theology, can we begin to construct an ecclesiology that will allow us, in some partial and fragmented way, to name the ekklesia in our midst.[7]

Pictures of Women

Picture One

Sue belongs to an independent African American church and came to seminary right after college. In seminary she has experienced black church studies and feminist studies as two arenas, often divided. Though extremely committed to a womanist theological perspective, she now debates how far she should push her views in the church. The black church is her home, and yet it is not very receptive to her concerns as a woman. At the independent church to which she belongs, no woman, as of yet, has been ordained. Sue wants to pursue ordination but is concerned that even as an ordained woman, she may find it difficult to pursue her interests in womanist theology. Yet she knows that ordination will give her access to privileges of leadership and that her very presence will challenge the patriarchal structures of authority. Furthermore, Sue is deeply committed to the role the black church has played in the African American community to which she belongs and is convinced that the church must continue its role as a community of justice and deliverance in the United States.

This first picture raises the question of the symbolic reality of ordination. As Anne Carr has observed, the refusal to ordain women symbolizes the exclusion of women from decision making on the basis of ascribing inferiority to women.[8] Whatever one thinks of ordination, and some feminist positions question the validity of ordination, the present practice of keeping women from it symbolizes the patriarchal oppression and belittlement of women in the church. The inclusion of women in ordained ministry is, in a sense, only one litmus test of how far the present ecclesia can move.

This picture also represents the deep commitment that many women have to the church as a space of justice and community and as a force of real political presence, at least in certain contexts. The frustration of the injustice of the lack of ordination of women and the inability of the church to advocate certain forms of justice is a lived reality for many women. The internal contradiction between the church as a voice of justice and as a barrier to justice sets the agenda for many women (and men) in theological education. Sue and many others like her want desperately to work within the structures of the organized church. With deep feelings of belonging to a particular church home, of loyalty to a particular tradition, Sue wants only to continue the mission of the church within its officially sanctioned ministry.

Picture Two

Paula is a United Methodist second-career woman with both a graduate degree and years of experience in clinical psychology. She abounds with theological talents, pastoral skills, organizational abilities, and pure human energy and vision. Paula is in a committed relationship with another woman, and thus has had to face the questions of ordination in a mainline Protestant church that refuses to ordain "self-avowed" gay, lesbian, and bisexual Christians. Paula has decided to follow her calling into a nonconventional ministry, not only because of the denomination's refusal to ordain her but because she increasingly questions the mainline church's failure to care, in any genuine way, for physical bodies. Deeply interested in spiritual practices that connect one to God, self, and others, Paula believes that only in new forms of community can Christians realize, in this day and age, the living traditions of Christian spiritual practices in worship, contemplation, and service in and through the body of the earth and through persons' bodies.

This picture illustrates women's ability to move outside the present forms of the church to other types of ministry. It also represents the fact that women, and men, move into para-institutional forms of church for reasons other than mere ordination issues; they also move because denominational churches too often fail to live unto the gospel they proclaim. In a world of great crises and suffering, too many churches offer worn-out, ritualized answers to questions that no one asks. In a day of incredible need, when bodies hurt, suffer, and die, when even the earth's body is dying, the denominational churches seem not to speak and act. In new communal spaces, women and men "re-vision" tradition in order to worship, to pray, and to serve. Paula, and many like her, know that Christian community can and must exist. She represents many in our churches and in theological education who wonder if they are not living in the midst of a "paradigm change" of institutions and ideas of Christian practice.[9]

Picture Three

In a ceremony sponsored by a women's group in the university, a rite of healing is offered. This ceremony adapts a Christian liturgical format for the healing of women violated in rapes and other forms of assault. Several women rise and tell their stories of being raped and abused. Each woman describes the attack, each woman talks about her feelings, and each woman talks about the long journey of healing that followed. Women who have suffered rape and abuse are invited to come forward and symbolically wash away the defilement they feel and recall again the experience of new birth, hope, and grace. The ceremony is a profoundly moving and deeply religious event.

The experience stays with me for days, as I reread time and time again Rita Nakashima Brock's *Journeys by Heart.* "The Christa/community of erotic power is the connectedness among the members of the community who live with heart. Christa/Community evidences heart, which is the conduit in human existence of erotic power."[10] Brock reclaims the notion of eros, so feared and ridiculed as lust and uncontrollable sexuality, to speak of the primal energy of created interconnectedness. Erotic power is embodied, relational, and synergistic. It is this "erotic" power that flows in all our connections with God, with each other, with earth, and this power is far more fundamental than our divisions, our hierarchies, our dualisms. This erotic power, seen by Brock as the fundamental connection of Jesus and communal redemptive existence, or what she calls Christa/Community, heals brokenness, even the brokenness suffered by the most vulnerable.

Rita Brock's notion of the presence of erotic power in Christa/Community makes sense in the context of this worship service. It gives words to name the power that women felt in the presence of the corporate, embodied healing. For the connection experienced by the women present at that service of healing was the divine embodied energy that allowed healing to be claimed.

Picture Four

Some years ago a woman student wanted to sponsor spirituality groups for women as a third-year ministry project. We spent the summer planning the groups. She gathered resources; I tried to convey that even if only a small group showed up, it was a valid project. She went to the first meeting, ready to meet with twelve women; there were over fifty. These spirituality groups continue today, some for women only, some for men only, some for mixed groups. They are self-directed, with participants deciding their own process. Some of these groups rely on spiritual disciplines and liturgies they adopt from Christian traditions; some compose new liturgies and disciplines; still others combine past and present liturgies and disciplines. Some of these groups operate through a process focusing on open communication; others tend to concentrate on a process of physical movement and embodiment. Some access spirituality through creative visualization and imagination, and others combine various processes to be a spiritual community. They are spaces in which many students in the seminary in which I teach experience church.

Without viewing them through the lens of feminist theology, such spirituality groups may simply appear to be students entertaining themselves, the seminary attempting to address the spiritual needs of the students, or small groups formed for religious self-help. Such dismissals can be heard from faculty, students, and church persons. But another way to look at these groups is that they are church—they express, represent, and constitute the nature and reality of church. If one agrees, as do students participating in those spirituality groups, that church is where the Spirit is present, then these groups, at least in some partial way, must be considered church.

Such pictures are not the only ones that might be shared to illustrate the reality of feminist practices of theological education around the challenge and possibility of church. But these pictures serve, minimally, to allow us to ask questions about what is the reality of church for those women and men who participate in feminist theological education.

1. Why shouldn't women be ordained? For the majority of Christians, women still cannot be ordained in their denominations. Almost all Christian denominations refuse ordination to self-avowed lesbians and bisexual women.
2. Why should women want to be ordained? Is the clerical caste itself a part of the problem, or how can the ordination of women (all women?) transform the nature of ordination itself?
3. What is the purpose of the church and where do we really experience church?
4. What are liturgies of remembrance and imagination? Do they include rites of healing for abuse victims?
5. What is the relation between women experiencing Christian community and the official church structures?
6. How do we decide what is church, ekklesia, corporate redemptive existence?
7. What is the role of the church in the world?

We can multiply the questions almost endlessly, since the point is that women's varied experiences of ekklesia are a resistance within existing church structures, an alternative to present church structures, and a transformation of church structures. Feminist practices of ekklesia are, above all else, new understandings of what counts as church.

Women-Church

This reality of church in feminist liberationist Christianity is often called "women-church." The term arose among women whose "inclusion" in issues of ordination has consistently been forbidden: the Roman Catholic women's movement in the United States. Elisabeth Schüssler Fiorenza used the term *ekklēsia gynaikōn* to assert that women are church "and have always been church."[11] Diann Neu translated this term as "women-church," and the term was adopted by a coalition of Roman Catholic women's groups holding a common conference in 1983. Since that time, the term has been broadly used to mean that women's reality—experiences, relationships, practices—is and has been and will be church.

I think about it in terms of visual images. For years, as a theological student, whenever I heard the term *church* I was confused. Does this term mean first of all the major church councils? Does "church" refer really to denominational structures? Or is the real meaning of "church" the policy and discourses produced by the official leaders? Does it mean public worship conducted by the solemn clergy over the heads of the people?

Or does "church" signify what I see a great deal of: women in the church, making the meals, active on boards, going into homes when needed, composing the majority of worshipers on Sunday morning? What is the meaning of church, the theology of ecclesiology, if one examines what Mary Ann Zimmer has termed the domestic work of the congregations, the religious practices of those who do not belong to the clerical knowledge class?[12] As with all concepts, how you image reality through the concept orients you to certain meanings.

This is an extremely basic and important point, though we have been taught to think of "church" as the official actions to such an extent that we overlook the church of the people, especially the women. I have often been a part of discussions of how to make the church inclusive of women. On the one hand, I know that this means access to official language, ordination, leadership—the right to have a say in determining what matters. On the other hand, the comment always somewhat startles me, since for most churches women dominate the membership.

Women-church names a reality already among us and considers it as important and as real as any other reality. Yet women-church not only opens the lens but casts a critical look through the reality of women in the church. It stands as a critique of denominational policy about and practices concerning women and a resistance, even an alternative, to them. To say it differently, denominational boundaries do not define the church. The ekklesia exists where the Spirit is present, where the Spirit works through the lives of women and men for the realization of new life for all, including the earth.

What women and men experience through feminist practices of theological education is not only the critique of current church structures, but new spaces of a transformed and transforming ekklesia. The women who participate in the rites of healing, the women and men who partake of spirituality groups and the additional practices through feminist courses, work groups, retreats, and so on, experience ekklesia. This ekklesia is not limited to theological education, though that is the focus of this book. The boundaries are fluid in this ekklesia, as it relates to local congregations and denominational structures. This ekklesia is the theological naming of the feminist liberation movement of Christianity as it exists as communal redemptive existence. In order to understand the reality, possibility, and challenge of ekklesia, it will be necessary to articulate, then, a theological discourse of ecclesiology.

An Ecclesiology

To seek clarity about church within feminist practices of theological education is to inquire about a construction of ecclesiology. Following our general method and the steps we have already taken to speak of the ekklesia, our reflections must be critical: based in actual reality of how both women and men struggle in religious communities, as well as upon their dreams and desires for ekklesia. In this sense, feminist ecclesiology is a theological discourse that seeks to express the present reality and to anticipate what ought to be the case.

Schüssler Fiorenza has spoken of this in terms of the "already" and the "not-yet" of the ekklesia of women. Feminist ecclesiology does not begin with the assumption that where the institution is, there is the church. Rather, it begins by seeking to name the church as that place which opposes patriarchy and which envisions new forms of flourishing, or what I shall speak of in terms of the denunciation of sin and the annunciation of grace.

The ekklesia is not identified, then, with separatist groups or with a church for women only. Rather, the ekklesia is that place of

God's redemptive presence where women and men can be emancipated from sin and transformed into freedom. In this sense, the ekklesia is defined by the presence of the Spirit.[13] Theologically speaking, the ekklesia is defined or identified by a theological norm. Thus, following Schüssler Fiorenza, I suggest the use of the term *ekklesia* instead of *women-church* as a way to signify the theological normativity of a feminist ecclesiology.[14]

Identifying the theological normativity of ecclesiology is especially important in feminist practices of theological education because women don't found a separate "church," via a separate institution parallel to that of denominations. Unlike the black church in America, feminist ekklesia does not have a separate geographical identification. What it does have are distinguishable theological and spiritual spaces of ekklesial community.

The theological space of ecclesiology in feminism will parallel two important places within "classical" Christian tradition. First, the centrality of ecclesiology is formulated through the notions of sin and grace, in which the church is understood to be the corporate nature of grace in the world. Friedrich Schleiermacher, for whom the church, sin, and grace are key symbols in theology, illustrates what it is that feminist theology resonates within the Christian theological tradition. For Schleiermacher, the experience of grace, indeed the reality of grace, is manifest through the corporate nature of the church. As Schleiermacher states in proposition 87 of *The Christian Faith:* "We are conscious of all approximations to the state of blessedness which occur in the Christian life as being grounded in a new divinely effected corporate life, which works in opposition to the corporate life of sin and the misery which develops in it."[15] Grace, the antithesis to sin, arises through the corporate reality of church. The church exists in the world as an antithesis to sin. Now certainly feminists have a different material understanding of sin and of grace than did Schleiermacher. But the formal parallel of defining ecclesiology not through individual piety or the handing down of tradition but through the antithesis of sin and grace is a shared understanding in Schleiermacher's symbolic patterning of "church" and in feminist ecclesiology.

Another aspect of Christian tradition that helps explicate how feminist ecclesiology functions in theology is the model of church as a sign in the world. Avery Dulles, in *Models of the Church*, explains that in this model the church is a visible sign of God's invisible grace.[16] But as a visible sign of invisible grace, the church attempts to be efficacious, deepening and spreading the effects and impacts of grace. This model was made famous by Karl Rahner and has been transformed by various Latin American liberation theologians. Gustavo Gutiérrez in *Theology of Liberation* argues that the church is the sacrament of God; that is, the church is identified wherever it is that God is manifest in history.[17] Gutiérrez insists that the sacramental definition works only as the church exits not for itself but for others, representing God's gratuitous activity in the world. God's activity is, according to Gutiérrez, to work against sin and for grace. Thus precisely as a sacrament for the world, the church, according to Gutiérrez, denounces sin and announces grace. He argues that the church does not exist for itself, and thus it is impossible to identify with the concrete walls. The church is that which manifests God's salvific activity by existing for others. The church is a visible sign of God's invisible grace.

In feminist theology operating in the North American situation, the notion of the ekklesia as a sign allows feminist theology to criticize existing churches of patriarchal idolatry. As a sign of salvific activity, the ekklesia also exists to embody redemptive existence, to anticipate new forms of flourishing. Sallie McFague has suggested that the church, or what I am calling the ekklesia, be a sign of the new creation:

> Where human beings, decentered as the goal of creation and recentered as those who side with the oppressed, create communities embodying concern for the basic needs of the life-forms on earth, aware of their profound interdependence as well as individuality, *here* is the church from the perspective of the organic model.[18]

A feminist ecclesiology creates discursive spaces to denounce sin and to announce grace. Since the ekklesia is a sign, all that it is and does functions to work against sin inside the church and in the society. Likewise the ekklesia functions to signify grace, to live in ways that image planetary flourishing.

Sin and Patriarchy

The present reality is distorted and depraved; it damages the self, it distorts community, it destroys relationship with the earth, and it disrupts communion with God. What women and men experience and learn in feminist practices of theological education is how to speak of the destruction and violation of creation, and how to anticipate new ways of human and planetary flourishing.

It is only very recently that feminist theologians have begun to elaborate on the denunciation of sin.[19] The doctrine of sin, though necessary in a Christian symbol structure, has been problematic for immediate feminist attention. The doctrine of sin, after all, has been used time and time again to configure women as somehow more sinful than men and has been gendered as female. In addition to the "feminization" of sin in Christianity, modern theology shrank and emptied the notion of sin of any substantive content. The existentialist-influenced theologians argued that sin had to do with individual anxiety and epistemological limitations. American neoorthodoxy informed us that, realistically speaking, we just had to accept sin as it affected the social order. In addition to these theological reductions of sin, a kind of popular piety existed that identified sin with minor infractions of middle-class morality. Sin seemed to have little to do with combatting the enormous forces of personal, interpersonal, social, and global destruction.

There has been, however, an implicit doctrine of sin in feminist theology. Like other forms of liberation and prophetic theologies, feminist theology is predicated upon the assumption that something is dramatically wrong with contemporary existence. Most specifically, sin is identified with patriarchy. As we have already seen, patriarchy is, to quote Schüssler Fiorenza, "a differentiated political system of graduated domination and subordination that found its classic Western legitimization in the philosophy of otherness."[20] That feminist theology finds patriarchy as the disordering of creation rests on feminist theology's notion of the goodness of human beings, of the earth, of the created order (the doctrine of creation); the possibility of transformation (salvation and redemption); and other symbols of Christian discourse. Ecclesiology is formed, at least in part, through these symbols that name God.

Feminist theology speaks about what Christian theologies have almost always spoken about: sin that infects and distorts the human condition. Naming the infection, distortion, and disordering of sin opens up, as we shall see, spaces of grace as transformation: justice, community, and spirituality. To speak of sin is, almost by definition, central to the symbolic grammar of Christianity. The need to articulate a discourse on sin exists not merely because we are "required" to do so out of the tradition or out of our own spiritual experience but because a discourse of sin enables us to name the many dimensions and elements of patriarchy and phallocentrism. This discourse of sin allows us a way to talk about the depth ordering and small capillaries of oppression, the many ways that patriarchy causes suffering in the social order and of its destructiveness in various forms of subjectivity.

Feminist theology, in the practices of theological education, constructs a new doctrine of sin that names women's work against patriarchy and for survival and flourishing. But in this construct, feminist theology is not just an adaptation of secular views of patriarchy and phallocentrism. For in the mutual transformation of sin and of patriarchy, what is constructed is a way to speak about the many ways in which oppression occurs and about the continual production of oppression through patriarchal structures and practices. Indeed, patriarchy is revealed not simply as a social arrangement nor as individual acts of cruelty toward women on the part of men but rather as a deep spiritual ordering that invades and spreads across the social order—through individual identity, to social practices, to lines of authority in institutions, to cultural images and representation.

One of the most frequent, and disturbing, symbols of sin for women is rape. Every time I have a course in feminist theology, women, and occasionally a man, talk about rape: their experiences of it, their continual fear of it, their understanding of it through Christian symbols. I have now learned to expect one phrase I have heard from every woman: "I have never spoken of this in church." The reality and/or fear of rape is one of the most fundamental realities for many women. Rape, for women, forms how we feel about ourselves, how we understand the connections and boundaries between ourselves and others, how we experience and speak of God.

What does it mean to take rape as a symbol of sin within feminist theology? Viewed through sin, rape is seen as a complete distortion of relationship, as the mockery and devastation of what religiously "relationship" might mean. The betrayal of creation and the refusal of any sense of covenental relationship, rape physically, emotionally, culturally, and structurally wounds the innocent victims and alienates the humanity of the perpetrator. Rape is not just a legal and psychological act; it is a spiritual act in which the connectedness of humans with one another and with God is violated and broken, and the reality of defilement, guilt, responsibility, terror, alienation, and separation will take years and years to be made whole again. As Marge Piercy points out in "Rape poem," rape names the ontic condition under which most women live most of the time:

Fear of rape is a cold wind blowing
all of the time on a woman's hunched back.
Never to stroll alone on a sand road through pine woods,
never to climb a trail across a bald
without that aluminum in the mouth
when I see a man climbing toward me.[21]

If sin helps us to name the reality of rape, the reality of rape also helps us to symbolize sin. Throughout history Christians have had different ways to speak of reality and effects of sin: disease, burden, debt, defilement, immoral acts. Rape is yet another way to speak of sin, one that speaks both of reality and effects. As a naming of the reality of sin, rape symbolizes that sin is sometimes incurred not through individual acts (in terms of the victim); that sin is something that is done to us and still carries the effects of defilement, woundedness, and terror. In many Christian traditions, sin symbolizes broken relationship with God, self, and others, and so also does rape signify, even as it creates brokenness and disruption. Finally, rape reminds us of the double-sidedness of so much sin: personal and cultural; existential and structural. Rape is an individual act: an act of violence by one person against another. But rape is also cultural and structural: it is perpetrated in times of war as a common act against the enemy and it is, at least in the United States, currently a cultural epidemic. The double-sidedness of rape as sin reminds us that we no longer can work out of an isolated anthropology: we are interrelated by nature and culture, that for what one person does, another bears the cost.

The denial of rape, the refusal to speak about rape, especially in Christian churches, reminds us of shared complicity, of refusing to offer grace and healing in sin, of refusing to listen to victim-survivors tell the truth. Instead the sin of rape is extended as we run the other way. Toni Morrison makes this kind of observation at the end of *The Bluest Eye*, a novel about a young woman's rape and impregnation by her father, "We tried to see her without looking at her and never, never went near. Not because she was absurd, or repulsive, or because we were frightened, but because we had failed her."[22]

The ekklesia denounces sin as that which breaks relationships with God, with others, with ourselves, with the earth.[23] The ekklesia is the corporate existence that provides us with the space and the resources to work against the disordering and destruction of the created good. As such, sin may be defined as *depravation*, a corruption

that destroys the very conditions of survival. Sin is also *deprivation,*
the loss that prevents human flourishing. Sin distorts and destroys
our ability to survive and to dream, to make the necessary conditions of life, and to flourish within these conditions.

The ekklesia provides us at least three spaces in which to name
and oppose sin: the space of lamentations of suffering; the space for
critical analyses of systems of oppression; and the space in which to
interpret the depth order of sin as idolatry. Within the corporate
space of the ekklesia, feminist theology names as concretely as possible the events in which life is distorted and prevented from flourishing. It is extremely important, given the reification of patriarchy
throughout most of Western history, that women be allowed to cry
out and to lament in concrete and detailed ways the experiences suffered. The widespread use of poetry, arts, and fiction in feminist theology classes, for example, has in part to do with this aspect of
lamentation: the wailing and groaning in travail over the distortions
of creation. This breaks through the denial of suffering and of oppression in our ordinary church practices and encourages persons to
tell the truth about their lives. Spaces for lamentation enable persons
to reflect on their lives in new, honest ways.

The rite of healing in the worship service of healing that we discussed in picture two was in part concerned with creating a space
for lamentation: being able to wail and weep and speak the truth in
the context of religious community. Rosemary Radford Ruether's
Women-Church includes a litany about rape that blends telling this
truth with the truth of the psalmist. After initially introducing the
rape victim-survivor, a group responds:

> My God, My God, why have you abandoned me? I have cried
> desperately for help, but still it does not come. During the day
> I call to you, my God, but you do not answer. I call at night but
> get no rest.[24]

As this litany suggests, lamentation is essential to the psalms: the
wailing and groaning in travail is the truthful examination and expression of one's life.

A second dimension of the ekklesia is providing space for the
critical analyses of systems of oppression. Perhaps the contribution
of liberation theologies to the "history" of the doctrine of sin will be
that sin is structured through social order, through interpersonal relations, and through "forms of subjectivity," psychological structures available at a given time. These critical analyses seek to
understand internal and external oppression. Sin, as we shall see in

the third aspect, continues its ongoing mutation and patriarchal oppression, continually finding new ways of snaking through existence. Therefore, it is necessary to develop new critical analyses
focusing on political, economic, psychological, cultural, and linguistic structures of oppression. This is not to reduce sin to such systems,
but rather to analyze how sin is expressed, extended, and even mu-
tated through these systems.

The ekklesia is a space of dialogue between feminist theology
and other forms of theory, including the whole range of feminist theories. Since "sin" can no longer be considered utterly separate from
the social and cultural orders in which we live, it is necessary for
theology to engage other forms of theory to analyze how sin is structured and transmitted. Such dialogue includes the work of feminist
theologians with ecological theory and the natural sciences, as in
Sallie McFague's *The Body of God* and the work of feminist theologians with public policy and the social sciences, as in Pamela D.
Couture's *Blessed Are the Poor?*[25] Critical analyses must include in-
vestigations into the interstructured oppression of racism and sexism through the arenas of aesthetics, economics, politics, science,
and religion, such as the understandings offered in Delores
Williams's *Sisters in the Wilderness*.[26] Using such books is just one
way for the ekklesia to provide space for teaching about and working against systems of distortion and destruction.

The third dimension of the ekklesia in relation to the denunciation of sin involves providing spaces in which to interpret what I call
the depth ordering, or the continual process of producing and re-
producing sin. Sin is not static; rather, there is an ongoing generation
and even mutation of sin. This notion of the continuing produc-
tion/reproduction of sin has long been pointed to in Christian theology through notions such as demonic powers or human biological
reproduction, notions no longer credible. Perhaps the best that we
can offer about the ongoing generative power of sin is what Paul
Tillich called the Fall as a halfway myth; that is, the best we can do
is persuasive description rather than adequate explanation of how
sin started.[27]

The depth order of patriarchy might be called "phallocentrism,"
by which I mean the logic of the representation of the genders (what
is woman, what is man) through a particular construct of masculine
identity and desire. If patriarchy has to do with the actual ordering
of subordination and control, phallocentrism, or the depth ordering of
sin, has to do with the often anonymous logic behind this ordering. The most powerful example of "logic" of language following

phallocentrism is in a story told to me by an obstetrics nurse and divinity student. The nurse said that in the nursery of the hospital in which she worked, boy babies were placed in bassinets with blue cards that said "Hi! I'm a boy!" and girls were placed in bassinets with pink cards that said "It's a girl." Phallocentrism constructs the boy in the dominant subject position and locates the girl as an object. As the children grow older, phallocentrism will mutate in all sorts of ways: boys will be spoken of as aggressive, strong, independent, and girls will be awarded the adjectives of quiet, well behaved, soft-spoken. When they are older still, boys will be offered a sexuality portrayed through the masculine gaze, as the one who objectifies and conquers; girls will find their sexuality represented as that which is posed and observed. This depth order of phallocentrism will mutate into all sorts of forms. Men will lose connection with feelings in order to subject the world unto themselves. Women will feel lesser than men, will worry about being impostors if they are successful, and no matter what their position or occupation, will try to live within the masculine gaze. This ordering will make its way through language, subjectivity, and politics. Of course, individual women and men will be exceptions to the mutating power of the phallocentrism, but such men and women will live on the boundaries of the cultural norm.

This depth order of sin has to do with establishing patterns and identities of separation and hierarchies of control. Going back to the basic definition of sin as out of relationship, the depth ordering of sin names a pervasive pattern or logic of keeping persons and creation in their defined place so relations cannot and will not be formed. Phallocentrism involves hidden rules: rules of seeing groups of persons in terms of differences as always oppositional and then ordering these differences by principles of superior/inferior and subjectification/objectification.[28] It is important to point to this depth ordering in order to monitor the continual mutations of sin. Patriarchy and phallocentrism can not be fixed on any one instance or expression; they are the ongoing pattern of objectification and control represented by the signs assigned to babies even before they leave the hospital.

Within feminist theology, this continual phallocentric ordering in language, in politics, in personal structures of identity has deep resonances with the notion of idolatry. Idolatry, within Christianity, has to do with the daily structures and practices of following false gods. Patriarchy with its ordering of phallocentrism becomes, quite literally, the false god that is trusted and submitted to, and to which the sacrifice of human victims are offered. This idolatry distorts all possible relations with each other, with God, with ourselves, with the earth. Sacrifice is made to this idol through the destruction of the conditions of the earth and especially the "others" of history.[29]

Thus the ekklesia as a manifestation of God, as a visible witness of grace, denounces sin. This means that the ekklesia provides spaces and discourses for lamentations, that its "walls" stand to open up human hearts and to let persons wail. The ekklesia also takes as its responsibility the analysis of structures of oppression, revealing how systems of distortion, destruction, and violence work. The church speaks out about the ongoing generation of sin, trying to describe the generating practices of oppression.

Ekklesia of Grace

But as the ekklesia denounces sin, it announces grace, new ways of human and planetary flourishing. Martin Luther was fond of observing that we only understand the reality of sin when we receive grace. Since the ekklesia not only denounces sin but announces grace, it exists to be a space in which persons find new forms of relating, in which new discourses are formed, in which new experiments of transformation take place. The church is, as Schüssler Fiorenza has observed, real and anticipatory: it already has the traces of new ways of being and doing, and it continuously creates, experiments, forms, and dreams new possibilities.[30]

The ekklesia exists as the space of grace, the grace that enables and empowers humans to form new relations. Feminist practices of theological education unfold the ekklesia as spaces of grace for experiencing and creating new forms of relationships with God, self, others, and the world. These relations may be personal, interpersonal, or structural. What women and men experience in feminist ekklesia spaces is the power of grace, or, to use the words of Johannes Baptist Metz, grace as living differently.[31] As taught in the logic of Christian symbols, grace does not just complete a transaction out there, beyond the cosmic time, but it transforms us to live differently, what the pietist tradition calls "holy living." This holy living includes saving us from the ravishes of sin. So, for example, it may be experienced as a woman begins to accept and realize that she is worthy, that she is "equal" to men. Grace also empowers new forms of flourishing within Christian community and within the culture and world. There are three principles or aspects of ekklesia as the annunciation of grace: the counter-public sphere of justice, the community of friends, and the spirituality of connectedness.

The Ekklesia as the
Counter-Public Sphere of Justice

Perhaps one of the strongest effects of feminist practices of theological education is the force and focus of justice. Feminist reflection on theological education has been defined through a justice-based education. This perspective of the ekklesia as the counter-space of justice has two terms for clarification: justice and counter-public.

Justice, at least in modern American society, has usually been imaged through a paradigm of distribution. Robin Lovin summarizes this kind of definition: "Justice concerns the distribution of goods, rights, and responsibilities among the members of a community."[32] In modernity, justice is essentially a nonconstitutive act of community; that is, justice doesn't make up the real web of community, but instead it distributes the secondary affects and concerns. In modern American society, justice is primarily managed as a matter of the welfare state. For mainline denominations, justice is often expressed as a matter of charity, or distribution of surplus goods to the poor.

In recent years, both in American society and in mainline denominations, justice has had a different voice—a voice of representation, deliberation, even self-definition. Theorists refer to this as a communicative model of justice, one in which justice is about the rights and responsibilities of self-determination.

Iris Marion Young's book *Justice and the Politics of Difference* illustrates this fuller sense of justice as constitutive of community. For Young, justice is "coextensive with the political."[33] The political is the entire realm of human decision making: cultural meanings, institutional structures, social habits, all that humans in some way decide, shape, or form collectively. Young opposes the distribution paradigm of justice for two reasons. First, it fails to consider the institutional structures that determine distribution. Second, the language of distribution distorts nonmaterial goods and resources. Justice becomes a matter of ends and things, rather than of right relations and processes. Young shifts the concept of justice from distribution to procedural issues of participation in deliberation and decision making. Justice, in Young's view, names the process and relationship of a community:

For a norm to be just, everyone who follows it must in principle have an effective voice in its consideration and be able to
agree to it without coercion. For a social condition to be just, it
must enable all to meet their needs and exercise their freedom;
thus justice requires that all be able to express their needs.[34]

Feminist ekklesia implies this "communicative" notion of justice, relying on biblical, theological, and critical-theoretical resources
to become a just community, a community in which each participant
has a right to have a voice in self-determination and community determination. This notion explains why our first picture of the inclusion of women for ordination is an issue of justice. For where
women are not allowed a say in the determination of their community, that then is injustice. Injustice, according to Young, has to do
with oppression and domination.[35]

Schüssler Fiorenza is the feminist theologian who has most advanced this notion of justice as the determining character of ekklesia. She invokes the term *ekklesia* to mark the utter difference
between the church as a community of democratic participation, a
communicative concept of justice, and the patriarchal church of an
interlocking system of discrimination and subordination. In the
ekklesia, neither women nor men speak as one group; rather different groups, individuals, and coalitions all have an opportunity to
participate in the self-determination of community. The ekklesia
names an entirely different type of community than the patriarchal
church, one constituted through justice rather than one which distributes justice as crumbs left from the table.

Schüssler Fiorenza calls this a counter-public sphere, by which
she means an oppositional space to the dominant public sphere in
which the critique of patriarchy is generated and feminist visions
and interests are articulated.[36] For Schüssler Fiorenza, the ekklesia
as counter-public sphere must not imitate the logic of the public, and
thus simply reproduce the patriarchal constructions of identity.
Rather, the counter-public positions itself within a radical ethical-
democratic paradigm.

The notion of counter-public is used in feminist theory to indicate the spaces in which women in various ways have always participated in decision making and deliberation about their lives.[37] The
notion is used to indicate that the public sphere, and I would add the
public church, always made certain notable exclusions as to who had
a voice in the public. But in addition to this "exclusionary" public
sphere, there were always competing public spheres. For instance,

women's missionary organizations in various churches constituted one of the main areas of a counter-public sphere for women. The notion of counter-public resists the notion that there is one public, so to speak, by expressing the particular spaces of emancipatory movements in this country.

The significance of the ekklesia as counter-public sphere is twofold: its stress on justice as a normative process of ekklesia and its stress on justice as the defining mission of ekklesia. As a counter-public of justice, the ekklesia works to create larger relations of justice in the broader social order. Justice, in a sense, defines the mission and nature of the ekklesia.

The Community of Friends

One of the most genuine social, personal, and religious desires today is for community. In a highly individualized and rapidly transient culture, many women and men feel the loss of belonging to and being formed by a community. Certainly a consistent theme in Christian theologies is the importance, indeed often the priority, of Christian community.

Yet many forms and understandings of community tend to focus on homogeneity and closure, in which all persons are understood to be fundamentally "the same." In such homogeneous communities, meanings, behaviors, and practices are set; it remains only to apply and carry them out. As Michael Sandel has suggested, there are two fundamental types of community in modernity.[38] The sentimental community is composed of persons who, quite literally, all come from the same place. The associational community is simply an aggregate of individuals who meet together to satisfy some common interest.

The sentimental community has become both impossible and problematic. It is impossible because the physical conditions such as a stable population and relative self-enclosure of physical space no longer exist. The transient and largely urban nature of American society prohibits the set conditions of sentimental community. But such community is also problematic in that it excludes difference and openness as basic values and aspects of reality. Yet this type of community gives us the sense of belonging to and being formed by a community.

The associational community fails to provide this sense of belonging, even though it respects the autonomy of the individual. It, too, seems impossible for a multicultural society, since associational communities form relations between like-minded and equally abled persons. The problematic nature of this community has to do with its narrow representation and regulation of life.

Sandel has used the term *substantive* for another possible type of community. A substantive community is characterized by identity conceived of by its members. A community has substance in the sense that it has a fullness of relations determined through and through by the communicative sense of justice. In the pictures considered at the beginning of this chapter, all the women involved were both seeking and realizing the ekklesia as a real substantive community of justice and of the fullness of relations.

Perhaps it seems obvious that a community that fully includes women, as well as men, must be formed through justice. As women experience their right and power to speak, they begin to experience belonging with others. Women speak of it, often, in terms of truth telling—telling the truth about their lives. In modern church structures much goes untold: abuse, relationship problems, sexual orientation (other than the privileged type!), political opinions, and so on. But how can persons have any sense of belonging and connecting if these basic facts are hidden from others? Or as one woman student said to me in speaking about her recent divorce "I sit in church on Sunday morning worshiping the Ultimate Creator, Sustainer, and Redeemer of Life. I am acutely aware that the one thing I cannot do in that sanctuary is to tell the truth about my life. It drives me crazy that I have to lie about my life in this particular community."

In defining justice through communication and deliberation, the space of community of truth telling is opened up. This truth telling has been expressed time and time again within feminist liturgical practices that focus on healing from abuse, on divorce, on holy unions, on birthing. Truth telling also occurs in feminist spirituality groups. To tell the truth is not only a model for the ekklesia as it exists within itself but also involves telling the truth of society in the sense of denunciation of sin and critique of patriarchy. It includes a continual process of truth telling in a community itself and thus the stress on democracy as an ongoing deliberative process.

This substantive type of community, I think, names the distinctiveness of feminist ekklesia as community. Letty Russell writes of this relation of substantive community and justice in images of round table connection, kitchen table solidarity, and welcome table partnership.[39] Russell argues that community in the substantive sense is guided by the norms of the inclusion of others.

It is its substantive nature intertwined with spirituality that allows the church to be imaginative, creative, artistic, the purveyor of experiments in community. Of course, American utopian experiments were often religious, and in a very important sense, perhaps these utopian experiments represent the best sense of Christian community in the ability to anticipate and envision new forms of flourishing. Being honest about our lives, and having present a space of truth telling, engenders community as a space for the creation of new possibilities.

I have chosen to label this aspect of the church of grace a community of friends. The notion of friends is an important theme in feminist theology. Friends are those to whom we tell the truth and with whom we dream. Friends sustain a community continually open to change and transformation, that creates us but in turn that we always are in the process of creating. Friendship is a metaphor from the Christian tradition used to speak of human relationships with God. Thomas Aquinas, for example, broke with the Aristotelian tradition that allowed friendships only with those like us. He argued that friendship characterizes the life of charity.[40] He suggests that charity signifies not only a love of God but a love within God. The friendship between God and humanity involves a kind of intimacy with God that in turn confers a wisdom. What Thomas Aquinas rightly says is the nature of friendship is a loving with, an actualizing of the connections that in turn create in the participants greater wisdom.[41]

The feminist stress on friendship is an apt characterization of the substantive nature of the community. For friendship affords the intimacy that allows us to speak and hear the truth of our lives, that gives us the moral imagination to create visions of what ought to happen, that allows the flourishing that ought to exist. The familiar conversation that constitutes love with God characterizes life within the ekklesia.

Spirituality as a Praxis of Connectedness

Perhaps one of the richest aspects of feminist practices of theological education is the spirituality in the ecclesia. By spirituality I mean the actual lived experience of individuals and communities, our way of being and doing in the world. In feminist practices of ekklesiality, spirituality is a praxis, a way of living. Spirituality as a praxis is invoked and created in part by the symbols and doctrines, in part by the rituals and community. Feminists often use the metaphor of the web to connote spirituality, for the metaphor points to spirituality as that web of connectedness of all that we are and do and to the ongoing intentional activity. Spirituality, in a very real sense, is not what we have but what we do and who we are in the ongoing web of connections.

This fundamental definition of spirituality in a feminist view has been made especially clear by the feminist ecological theologian Sallie McFague in *The Body of God*. McFague argues that it is the reality of connectedness that leads both to a natural piety and to ethical response, which in turn is rooted in an appreciation of creation.

> It is, finally, at a deep level, an aesthetic and religious sense, a response of wonder at and appreciation for the unbelievably vast, old, rich, diverse and surprising cosmos, of which one's self is an infinitesimal but conscious part, the part able to sing its praises.[42]

As McFague points out, this spirituality includes an attitude of piety and an ethical response. The ethical response is to live in respect for the differences and the diversity of the creation, to help the planet and humans to flourish, and to tend the connections within which we live. The relation of ethics, aesthetics, and religious senses produces certain spiritual values. These values are mutuality, embodiment, and openness.

The value of mutuality carries the explicit connotation of being in relationship with others and with God as the horizon within which we live. Traditionally, this value of mutuality has been considered as an inherent female trait; women's ability to care and nurture has been understood as biologically, psychologically, and socially determined. Feminists, critical of the ideological distortion involved in structuring both psychologically and politically women's sacrifice of the self, seek to reconstruct mutuality as a foundational value in reality. It is out of mutuality that self arises. Mutuality names the fundamental relation of God and world. Thus feminists invoke the notion of God's relationship to the world as being that of friend rather than of sovereign.

The second value is embodiment or corporeality. Nature and history are not finally separable. Humans realize and recognize nature through historical experience, but likewise, historical experience has its matrix in nature itself, a nature that is more than any given experience. Feminist theologies speak strongly of creation and of new creation, calling us to live the Christian life within the context of nature. As we saw with Paula, to care for bodies, including the body of the earth, is the deepest and most fundamental aspect of spirituality as survival in the present situation. Spirituality is the nature and name of the survival of God's creation, of our creation, of the earth and all that is in it.

The spirituality of embodiment has to do with how we experience the vitality of God's spirit within us and within the creation in all that we do in Christian life. For instance, a spirituality of embodiment can be learned in the context of preaching, and perhaps even in preaching classes! A feminist teacher of preaching told me that in workshops on preaching she often had preachers, all women, first try to be in touch with their bodies, and with God through their bodies. In the chapel she would have the students feel their bodies, move around in the room and experience the spirit in different places, feel the energy and power of God quite physically in their bodies. And then she would invite the women to preach.

A spirituality of embodiment stresses an attentiveness to, but not a romanticization of, the body. The body can hurt and be hurt, it can curtail our activities and limit our thought and even our prayers; it forms our world. Another woman, once a student of mine, preached a sermon on how Christians do not have an able-bodied God as their primal image.[43] She preached while seated, and her body, differently-abled, pointed to and represented that of which she spoke: God whose body is known in brokenness, in suffering, in what would be considered an unconventional body. Those in the room thought in new ways of God's own embodiment in Jesus Christ, and likewise, in this context, of the nature of our own embodiment as the material of God's word that day. A spirituality of embodiment means that we attend to all bodies in their differences and that we attend to our own embodiment as loci of God.

Finally there is the value of openness, especially openness to difference and diversity. Certainly openness as a spiritual value has been well represented in modern theology. Karl Rahner's theological anthropology of openness to the ultimate mystery is his most fundamental religious value.[44] And Peter Hodgson makes openness a preferred term when he suggests that openness rather than ultimate concern is his definition of religion.[45] The feminist value of openness, as constituted through spiritual practices, encourages openness in terms of the process of embodiment of all connections. In the counter-public of the church, openness means realizing that deliberative rhetoric, the ongoing debate about our concerns and interests, is a process always open to change and negotiation. In the community of friends, openness means to deeply respect the ongoing process of friendship, where one may take various roles and identities, and move closer or further away in friendship.

Yet the connectedness of feminist spirituality must not be envisioned as a fusion of sameness. The power of connectedness exits in the ability to relate through differences, not sameness. As Susan Brooks Thistlethwaite has argued in *Sex, Race, and God,* the metaphors of connections and webs tend to be associated with white women's class and race privilege.[46] Thistlethwaite suggests that white women too often invoke the metaphors of connections and webs in order to stress bonding and warmth and to overlook difference and conflict.

I take Thistlethwaite's comments to raise the crucial question of the meaning of the term *connection.* For the warmth and bonding she identifies is in fact merely the continuation of what was allowed and expected of white women in patriarchy. The connections that feminist theology seeks are connections that relate through differences and that bring survival and flourishing together for all. In a sense, connection is the description of reality, a description not of warmth and bonding, but of conflict, of tension, of difference, of relatedness.

In my judgment, the term *connectedness* is decentered in any connotations of fusion and warmth through understanding it within the perspective of social naturalism. By social naturalism I mean a feminist naming of reality that brings together both is and ought, fact and value, within feminist theology.[47] Naturalism is a philosophical view emphasizing that human beings are undeniably connected to their surroundings.[48] For the naturalist, the very condition of our action, our being in the world, is our shared environment. Naturalism, at least as conceived in feminism, is conceived as open, plural, and diverse. A social naturalism connotes the complex relatedness of evolution, biology, social structures, languages, and so on.

A spiritual praxis of connectedness and embodiment seems, in my judgment, necessary to counter the patriarchal spirituality of detachment and separation. Christian spirituality has often been understood to be at its highest point with various forms of total detachment: from the body, from the earth, from the other. In patriarchal spirituality, transcendence as the highest value occurs only through separation from others and control of the body. A spiritual praxis of connectedness is that which both heals and resists patriarchal spirituality.

Conclusion

Feminist practices of theological education include a central focus on ekklesia and the development of an ecclesiology. As we have seen, writings on theological education have almost all carried some claim about the importance of "church" and "ecclesiology" for understanding theological education. In the books by Farley and Kelsey, that serve as the interlocutors of this text, reflection on the church as ecclesia or as congregation serves as a defining characteristic of theological education.

What this chapter brings to the forefront in terms of ecclesiology and theological education is not the mere importance of church, but the revisioning of the practice of ekklesia and the development of new discourses of ecclesiology. To signal this, I have chosen to use the term "ekklesia." It is important to understand that women and men who participate in feminist practices of theological education are engaged in a resistance to and transformation of what theological education has practiced and studied as "church."

I do not think that feminist practices of theological education are unique in their radical revisioning of ekklesial practice. African American students, both men and women, engage in African American ecclesial practices, reminding us that the dominant "church" has not been the only ecclesial structure in America. Students borrowing practices from other religious communities and bringing them into Christianity resist the judgment that such inclusion is non-Christian; they represent the church as a dialogical and inclusive community.

Nor is the revisioning and reforming of ecclesia and ecclesiology occurring only in theological schools. In local churches, in parachurch groups, in denominational structures, there appear to be different paradigms of ecclesia. Theological education both represents and contributes to broad changes in the ecclesia in North America. The multiculturalism within the churches of North America as well as worldwide requires and allows multicultural processes of theological education to develop.[49]

As students participate in feminist practices of ekklesia, the themes of justice, dialogue, and imagination again appear. Feminist practices of theological education entail understanding that education is not merely about or for justice; it is itself an activity of justice. Education is a process of forming the necessary conditions for persons to know and be able to articulate their needs and for persons to

learn the processes and ways of corporate life. In the educational traditions of the United States, education has almost always been seen
as related to the training of citizens for the democracy. Within this
historical context, feminist practices of theological education both
require and provide a process of education as an activity of justice.
As the authors of the Mud Flower Collective could say, "The fundamental goal of theological education must be the doing of justice."[50]

With an increasing commitment to a communicative instead of
a distributive model of justice, the educational process, as Sharon
Welch has said, "takes as its stand point the interaction between
'concrete others.'"[51] The theme of dialogue within the practice of
ekklesia-logy concerns learning to listen and speak with concrete
others in horizontal, rather than hierarchical, patterns of interaction.
Dialogue is thus necessary in the educational process, for justice will
not be served by harkening to the loudest voice or by allowing the
powerful to distribute the educational goods. Dialogue involves
learning how to become bicultural, to really hear the cultural experiences, beliefs, symbols, patterns of meaning in another person's religious experiences.

Justice and dialogue also require the imagination in order to develop new forms of flourishing. The stress on imagination and construction is central in feminist practices of ekklesia, from Schüssler
Fiorenza's stress on a hermeneutic that includes creative ritualiza-
tion or reconstruction to Brock's call for developing a Christa/
Community of erotic power.[52] Ecclesiology is about enabling the ecclesia to be about survival and flourishing in the present and future,
and for this, imagination is central in the quest for both justice and
dialogue.

4. The Warming Quilt of God: The Practice of Theology

When I first started to pull together my views of feminism and piece them together with the concepts of homiletics, it reminded me of the art form of quilting. It seemed to me that in writing this paper I was very much like the quilters who stitched pieces of materials together to form patterns for a quilt. As I meditated on this metaphor, I found that the metaphor of quilting resounded deep within me, and why not, for quilting is a beautiful metaphor to describe the connected, communal nature that to me is Christian feminist preaching. Just as women quilters gathered in groups and shared their life experiences with each other so does a Christian feminist preacher start with the communal sharing and claiming of women's stories. Just as the women quilters pieced their joys and sorrows, hopes and fears, into each quilt they made, so does a Christian feminist preacher piece together a sermon that is a quilt of shared stories, borrowed phrases, and materials from many lives and sources. Just as quilting was a communal act of love whereby the final product was given to those in need, a sermon is a communal act of spoken love, a conversation between the preacher and the congregation whereby the emancipatory transforming Word is given to a world so desperately in need of the warming quilt of God. In the art form of quilting there are as many styles and patterns of quilt making as there are courses at a seminary, but the quilt that I loved best and that best represents Christian feminist preaching is the quilt called the crazy quilt. Crazy quilts, scholars believe, were some of the earliest types of quilts. A crazy quilt is made from hundreds of scraps of material of all different sizes, textures, colors, and shapes. It is beautiful in its diversity. Having said this, I must also state that many people don't like crazy quilts because there is not a precise order and structure and pattern; it doesn't fit the norms. It was usually associated with people who were too poor to buy fancy materials, so they had to use scraps left over from worn out clothes to make the quilt. The crazy quilt represents what Christian feminist theology is about. The quilt itself represents the piecing together of our everyday experience in a communal act of love and the acceptance of all people and life experiences. It redefines beauty, and by redefining what is beautiful, feminist theology deconstructs and reorders values, norms, and structures.[1]

In this introduction to a paper for a class in feminist/womanist theologies, Megan Beverly captures the images of the work of feminist theology. What Megan specifies in feminist preaching applies to the broader context of feminist theology. For the work of feminist theology is about a communal act of sharing, about bringing disparate pieces together, about producing something for those in need, about sustaining a connection to what Megan Beverly so aptly calls "the warming quilt of God."

Megan Beverly's notion of quilting is used by many feminist theologians and theorists to describe their work. The distinctiveness of this metaphor names the reality of how women begin to experience the work and task of theology. Theology no longer uncovers unchangeable foundations or hands down the cognitive truths of tradition or discloses the classics or even figures out the rules of faith, as suggested by modern and contemporary metaphors of doing the work of theology. Rather, quilting, weaving, and constructing become the focus of theological work as a communal process of bringing "scraps" of materials used elsewhere and joining them in new ways.[2] As a first reading of this metaphor, the quilt stands for three interrelated dimensions of feminist theology: the work of theology, the symbols and narratives of theology, and the method or way of doing theology.

Feminist theology imaged as a quilt, or in other metaphors as weaving or reconstructing, is conceived as a work of emancipatory praxis. It is aimed at producing personal and social flourishing. As Beverly writes, "Just as quilting was a communal act of love whereby the final product was given to those in need, a sermon is a communal act of spoken love, a conversation between the preacher and the congregation whereby the emancipatory transforming Word is given to a world so desperately in need of the warming quilt of God." The work of theology is to contribute to the removal of oppressive structures, be they political, cultural, or personal, and it is to produce new visions of what life can be like. Theology is discourse about God in the Christian community, and as a discourse theology has specific functions or tasks. All theology speaks of God, Christology, ecclesiology, and in turn this discourse directs the praxis of the community. Within feminist theology the discourse of God directs the praxis of Christian community to emancipation: to be set free from sin and into new life.

Second, then, the metaphor of quilting calls attention to the images, symbols, and doctrines of theology through the work of emancipatory praxis. This occurs on a topical level when feminists reconstruct the symbols of God away from patriarchal images and ordering, or refashion the doctrine of the church as a space of self-determination. It also occurs when women and men envision language about God as itself emancipatory and seek to understand how theological discourse enables new ways of personal and social flourishing.

Envisioning the symbolic patterns of Christian theology is central to the historical role of Christian theology. Christian theologians have always been employed in interpreting tradition and in creating tradition, that is, in speaking to the specific needs of the day through fashioning the symbols and doctrines of the Christian faith. This is a dialectical or back-and-forth process. Through the symbolic lenses of Christianity we see reality, but reality in turn may lead us to refashion the meaning of basic symbols. By its very nature, theology focuses on the symbols and symbolic patterns of Christianity, and thus the imagination and aesthetics play an important role in feminist theology.

Third, as the quilt is created not simply to be looked at but to have a purpose, to work, it requires its own way or procedure of development and operation. The method of feminist theology has to do with "weaving" the symbolic pieces together. As Elisabeth Schüssler Fiorenza has pointed out, this method is rhetorical rather than "objective."[3] The guiding procedures for theological method include the deliberation of transformation, the honesty about reading from the present, and the integrity of persuasion. The metaphor of quilting allows an approach to resources of tradition that provides selection of materials for the patterning of the symbols of emancipatory praxis.

Quilting is one metaphor, but only one, to speak of the actual work of theology. Feminist theologians invoke metaphors of quilting or weaving because they underscore the history of women's lives in western culture, but also because they locate the very identity of theology in the context of functional warmth, of common beauty, of daily practices. "Reconstructing" is, as we shall see, yet another image, an image that is concerned with constructing theology in new ways. In the image of reconstructing, a double sense is invoked. In the first sense, reconstructing work means fashioning new spaces of survival and flourishing. And in the second sense, reconstructing invokes the role of imagination, the active sense of the theologian shaping as well as being shaped by Christian praxis.

Feminist theology is a reworking and reshaping of Christian practices within the context of the movement of feminist liberationist Christianity. As we have seen in previous chapters, the specificity of feminist theology arises out of the movement of women and men in theological schools and other ekklesial spaces, their spirituality, their quest for community and transformation, as well as their work with images, rationality, and praxis. This chapter interprets feminist theology in three basic steps: first, in terms of theology's contours and identifying characteristics; second, as invoking a new symbolic patterning of God; and third, as being constructed through rhetorical strategies around the norms of theology as saving work.

The Contours and Characteristics
of Feminist Theology

Theology is a practice, not merely a theory of abstraction, analysis, or explanation, at least in terms of how women and men participate in feminist practices of theological education. This statement is the conclusion I came to over and over again in interviewing students and faculty involved in feminist practices. One of the most frequent comments I heard was that of women who declared "I came to seminary to study theology, to learn how to do theology, not just to graduate." Most of these women did graduate, and many did enter into some kind of professional ministry, and almost all of them succeeded in using theological education to form themselves in the practice of theology. In actions and words as potent and creative as those offered by the recent authors writing on theological education and aiming their critique at the "clerical paradigm," these women and men attest that they simply are not interested in theological education as merely "professional training."

Of all the practices of feminist theological education, this is the most difficult for me to name because I am a professional theologian, trained in the methods and models of modern Western theology in which, as Farley and others have shown, theology is no

longer a form of wisdom, or a practice of Christian faith. I have had
to learn the lessons of theology as a particular *habitus* from students
and faculty over and over again. Students and faculty offered me
new lenses to see (and experience) what I call theology as saving
work, a practice that lies outside the parameters of modern theology,
but one that offers a material vision and an embodied wisdom for a
new form of Christianity in our day and age.

Perhaps the rather interesting irony and delightful possibility
within feminist practices of theological education exist most intensely, for me, in the practice of theology. As I indicated in chapter
1, the reformers of theological education who call for *habitus* have
only to look for its concrete sources within their schools: for students
engaged in feminist theology are, in quite specific ways, being
formed in theology as a practice, as a *habitus*.

In order for theology to emerge as a practice within feminist liberationist Christianity, attention must be paid to the agency of the
students, to the particular cultural issues and realities through
which theology emerges, and to the symbolic patterns of particular
Christian forms. In other words, the interpretive lens for theology
must focus on questions about agency, world, and symbol and how
they function together in a particular structure of Christianity.

Women and men engaged in feminist practices of theological
education embody specific cultural realities never before represented in theological education. To use ideas, symbols, concepts,
and narratives to craft one's life is, as we have seen, a matter of survival and flourishing, of trying to figure out how to bring together
cultural changes and one's personal life, communal realities and
new cultural environment. Theology as a practice of feminist liberationist Christianity means the dialectical relation of theory with action and action with theory, as well as the dialectical relation of
present (including the past) and future possibilities.[4]

In the first chapter of this book, we rehearsed some of the characteristics of "practice" as a socially shared behavior that provides
meaning and orientation to the world and that guides action. A practice offers its internal values and standards of excellence, and it is
done toward some end or vision. If theory, at least as usually conceived, involves abstract thought by the individual, the locus of
practice is the body of both the community and the individual participant. And practices, just as much as the idea, are the site of change
and transformation in Christianity.

How does theology function as a practice for women and men
in feminist theological education? For theology, at least as conceived

in much of modern theology, especially mid-twentieth-century modern theology, is about formal and/or existential "knowledge" (human and/or revealed) of the individual that has only secondary implications for agency and orientation to the world. Yet, for countless numbers of women and men engaged in feminist practices of theological education, theology is about "saving work," the emancipatory praxis of God and of Christian community in the world. To use the words of Catherine Keller, theology means the activity of "piling up together," which means "in community and solidarity gathering together resources for saving actions, refusing the ideologies of world-waste, woman-waste, people-waste, species-waste, by which we also waste whatever resources we may have as theologians."[5]

Students immersed in the ekklesia, religious communities of saving work, engage in denouncing sin and announcing grace. The point of Christianity is, in one sense, to pass on and work toward the radical transformation that the good news of Christianity brings. This participation in God's saving activity includes "work" that ranges from creating spaces of lamentations, to analyzing systems of distortion, to becoming friends with those in need, to experimenting with new concepts and forms of justice. Women and men engaged in feminist practices of theological education participate in the socially shared behavior of saving work.

But as we have also seen, men and women engage in the communal participation of saving work through the continual rewriting of their lives. Women's bodies, as we have seen, bear the marks and carry the testimony of vast cultural changes and social realities. Women's bodies also bear testimony to the possibility of survival, and even, at least sometimes, flourishing. Women, and men, who work on writing their lives in new ways, and engage in ekklesia, are formed in wisdom. Such wisdom includes new understandings and new ways of understanding the past and present, new images of the future, including the narrative future of the self, and new abilities to listen to the sufferings and the longings of others.

Feminist theology, then, is a way of understanding that itself seeks to be passionately engaged in saving work—the saving of the earth, of the oppressed, of humankind. The notion of theology as saving work suggests certain configurations of a model of knowledge as transformation for feminist theology. As a practice, theology includes transformation of social structures as well as transformation of personal narratives and of interpersonal relations.

This model of knowledge as transformation carries two important implications. First, knowledge is interconnected with other social forms. Knowledge is not about proving indisputable foundations from which all other forms of human activity can be traced. Rather knowledge, now often spoken of as discursive practices, is interlinked with other forms of human activity. Because of oppression and injustice, knowledge itself can and is faulted, linked with interest and power to create and continue hegemonic structures. As Edward Farley has argued in *The Fragility of Knowledge*, "a vision of corruption and redemption is the heartbeat of the Christian mythos," and this vision extends to and includes the various forms of knowledge.[6]

The second implication of knowledge as transformation is that knowledge as an understanding of God necessarily includes envisioning new possibilities for the social order, for relationships, for one's own life, and for the earth. Thus knowledge has an inherently imaginative aspect, with poetical, metaphorical, and narrative strategies seeking to provide new symbols, concepts, and theories to create and guide emancipation and transformation.

Feminist theology, then, employs a distinct type of knowledge, which I will call a *pragmatic critical theory*.[7] I use this term to name the project Cornel West outlines in his *The American Evasion of Philosophy* as he calls for a transformation of pragmatism into an explicit mode of cultural criticism.[8] Offering a selective reading of American pragmatism, West argues that American pragmatism opposed the nature of epistemologically centered philosophy with its spectator view of the human subject and understood philosophy as critical reflection on the problems of the age. Identifying pragmatism as a rich and diverse tradition characterized by future-oriented thinking, West defines pragmatism as "a cultural commentary or set of interpretations that attempt to explain America to itself at a particular historical moment."[9] Pragmatist philosophy arises out of the problems and dysfunctions of a particular situation and the desire that things can and must be different. As West says, "These efforts take the forms of critique and praxis, from that attempt to change what is into a better what can be."[10]

If pragmatism is a form of knowledge not about sure foundations but about cultural critique and transformation, critical theory marks the radicality of transformation needed. Pragmatism in its classical form under thinkers such as Charles Peirce and John Dewey tended to locally incorporate radical transformation but to work practically for correction of systems and structures. Dewey, especially, failed to connect his pragmatism to a symbolic form that would engender transformation, while Peirce, who provided a great deal of insight into symbolic transformation through his semiotics and metaphysics, failed to apply this to social and political transformation. Critical theory today plots the course of the more radical activity of joining symbolic, social, and personal transformation. Note, too, that the necessity for a pragmatic *critical theory* lies in part with the cultural struggles and needs for differences and pluralism to be built into theoretical models.

A critical theory, then, is the operation of knowledge for deliberation of the beliefs and activities in a community. As such, critical theories seek to uncover illusions, such as the socially constructed belief that it is natural for men to be superior to women. To state it even more strongly, critical theories uncover how discourses construct regimes of domination: how the discourse of men's natural superiority and of women's natural inferiority has functioned to justify the oppression, including the physical battering and rape, of women. Critical theory takes as its departure point the reality of oppression and suffering in society and attempts both to display the origin, function, and relations of structures that cause such oppression and to anticipate possibilities for change. Involved in both critique and transformation, imagination becomes central to the nature of critical theory.[11] To use the term employed at the beginning of the chapter, critical theorists are quilters using discrete pieces from various other fabrics and bringing them together to warm, protect, and add beauty, all the while deconstructing and reordering values, norms, and structures.

It may be helpful, at this point, to place feminist theology in the context of other popular theological models. For as we saw in the first chapter, ideas offer "competing" understandings of practices. These competing models serve as interlocutors, conversation partners in which various ideas are shared, revised, and even opposed to one another. The three models to which I will compare feminist theology are the deconstructionist, the hermeneutical, and the cultural-linguistic. In each of these comparisons I want to demonstrate both the agreements and disagreements of feminist theology with the model, as well as to show how the fundamental nature and task of feminist theology differs from each of these other three models.

The deconstructionist model can be exemplified by Mark Taylor's *Erring*, which proclaims the death of God, the disappearance of the self, the end of history, and the closure of the book.[12] Taylor contends that theology defines God as "presence" and argues that in postmodernity there is no such presence, there is only wandering or "erring." Taylor's reading of modern and classical theology is somewhat misleading, since God is never fully accounted for as present in modern theology. As Peter Hodgson has suggested, God is rather "appresented," appearing only through signs and symbols.[13] Taylor's deconstructive form of postmodern theology ends up having to proclaim the death of theology because it loses theology's ability to point to the transcendence and presence of God through the signs of the world. In Taylor's own words, "it would not be too much to suggest that *deconstruction is the 'hermeneutic' of the death of God*. As such, it provides a possible point of departure for a Postmodern a/theology."[14] In a sense, this way of understanding theology is the flip side of the modern understanding of modernity: that the other side of reason is irrationality or nonreason, that once man is gone there is death, and that there is no meaning in narratives or history if narratives and history themselves aren't secured.

Yet Taylor's position shares with feminism a critique of the binary logic and oppositional thinking prevalent in modernity, if not Western tradition. As a deconstructive enterprise Taylor's work is immensely helpful in that it demonstrates the binary ordering in the assumptions of modernity and what modernity fears will occur if this ordering is changed. God is God because God is not world; eternity is eternal because it is not time and thus not temporal. This kind of oppositional definition and binary ordering has functioned to create hierarchies in which the top term, and the group representing that term, receives most of the privileges in the social order. This is a theology that, in a sense, confronts the monsters of modernity's night directly and its solution is to transgress their origin and operation.

But this model focuses on theology as theory and seeks to explain, albeit in a deconstructive light, why former models of explanation are now no longer possible to maintain. It assumes, in a negative fashion, the primacy of "tradition"—that is, a set of texts—and views the symbolic construct of God as operating in an economy either of good or evil, transcendence or immanence. God may well operate this way in a particular construct of textual tradition, but what about the rituals and feasts? What about the prayers and practices of women? What about the subversiveness of slave narratives that did not transgress the master's Christian language, but carefully transformed it to make it expressive of African American religious praxis? Though feminist theology can use these "deconstructive" techniques of binary opposition, its fundamental assumptions about the nature of the problem and the nature of the solution are different from the epistemologically focused, tradition-bound theology of deconstructionism, at least in Taylor's variety. The nature of the problem in feminist theology is not the "unhappy consciousness of the historical agent" and the solution is not "profitless play."[15] Rather, the problem is far more massive and destructive: the corruption of knowledge and interest and power by those who seek to oppress and dehumanize those they classify as other. And the solution is not that of wandering around aimlessly, a solution only possible perhaps for those already privileged men who have the support to decry the self. Feminist theology propounds a response based in ethical commitment, a space including radical deconstructive analysis, but also the imaginative envisionment of human activity within the context of the struggles and desires of persons.

The opposite side of the coin, in contemporary theology at least, is the hermeneutical model of theology. The exemplary text here might be David Tracy's *The Analogical Imagination.*[16] Influenced by Hans-Georg Gadamer, Tracy argues that theologians begin within the tradition, that indeed the tradition itself forms our prejudgments. Indeed, understanding has a hermeneutical structure, with all understanding dependent upon tradition and prejudgments. Hermeneutical theologians such as Tracy focus on how we interpret the traditional texts, especially scripture, through a kind of back-and-forth dialogue between the text and our lives. This position highlights the creative activity of all interpretation, the nature of knowledge as dialogue, the openness within traditions to ongoing change and development.

There is a great deal of resonance between feminist theologians and hermeneutical theologians around the process of creative revisioning of the Christian tradition. Feminist theology, in general, differs from hermeneutical theology at two basic points. First of all, hermeneutical theologies tend to view the "Christian thing" as the Christian written tradition. In this model, the past reveals the truth to us and the theological task is to use the distance between the past and present to productively discover the truth. Feminist theology, on the other hand, understands the "Christian thing" to be the activity of emancipatory praxis as much in the present and future as in the past. Truth, in other words, has to do with saving work. Indeed, feminist theologians tend to view the "tradition" in terms of how texts functioned in historical situations as often counterproductive and even harmful to present and future "truth" of the survival and flourishing of women, and men, and the earth. The recognition that the past is represented too often through only the texts of those in power, with almost total silence from women and those who are deemed "others," tends to increase the suspicion that hermeneutical models can be used to protect the dominant cultural and political arrangements. This is not to discount the use of the "tradition" within feminist theology, but rather to dispute that the tradition has ethical or epistemological priority over present and future survival and flourishing.

The second difference that feminist theology has from hermeneutical theologies—and from deconstruction—is that the model of understanding is not one of praxis. As Werner Jeanrod has noted, Tracy does include ethical reading and judgment, but only *after* interpretation. Indeed Tracy states: "Ethical judgments seem far more appropriate *after* the interpretation of the 'world' of the work as a *possible*-mode-of-being-in-the-world."[17] For feminist theology, hermeneutics—the interpretive activity of theology—is included as part of the greater process of emancipatory praxis, one addressing the struggles and desires of this age through the anticipatory activity of the Christian feminist movement. Texts and other productions of the past will be used as material for critique, explanation, and even construction. But, as we shall see, the norms of theology come out of arguments aimed at the present and future activity.

In its stress on present and future saving activity as the focus of theology, feminist theology also differs from the third model, that of cultural-linguistic theology, for which George Lindbeck's *The Nature of Doctrine* can be used as a primary example.[18] This model focuses on a critique of foundationalism. This critique begins with the realization that there simply are no sure foundations, that all such claims are themselves metaphors born out of particular traditions of discourse. The foundationalist critique is an extremely important one in that it seeks to wrestle away from theology its accommodation to modern rationality. So powerful is this response in theology today that to be accused in academic circles of being a foundationalist is somewhat akin to being accused of being an inerrantist in liberal circles a generation ago.

If theology does not rest on an epistemological foundation, theology can be said to rest within a cultural-linguistic tradition. Lindbeck suggests that theology is a second-order discourse that provides the grammar of faith. This model assumes Christianity as a set tradition, codified or even guaranteed by determined boundaries. Theology's task is, as Ronald Thiemann argues, "to 're-describe' the internal logic of the Christian faith."[19]

Feminist theology differs from this theological model, first, in the stress on "re-description." Since for feminist theology the faith has itself been faulted and corrupted by patriarchy, the necessity is to transform faith away from patriarchal distortions. But feminist theology does share with the cultural-linguistic model a sense of symbolic logic of faith in the sense that the symbols of Christian faith provide the threads of continuity and transformation for piety, social witness, worship, the life of the community together, and life in the world. But the grammar, or the symbolic logic of Christian faith, is constructed in feminist theology through the understanding of emancipatory praxis and not, as in the cultural-linguistic model, through assuming a unified textual narrative that provides a kind of timeless grammar of faith. Claims that contemporary Christians must fit our stories into the biblical story fail to recognize what the hermeneutical and deconstructionist models make very clear: every reading of the biblical story is already our interpretation of various, often competing, texts to make a narrative.[20] Feminist theology thus departs from the cultural-linguistic model, as it does from the other two models, over the failure to place ethics as central to the very nature of theological understanding.

With all three models feminist theology has something in common. With the deconstructive model, feminist theology shares a strategy of "deconstructing" that which has been constructed through binary ordering. Feminist theology shares with hermeneutical theology a respect for dialogue and a willingness to risk continual reinterpretation of Christian symbols. The cultural-linguistic model and feminist theology agree that Christianity involves certain symbolic patterns as a kind of grammar or logic of the faith.

Yet feminist theology offers a very different understanding of the task and nature of theology. The task of theology, within feminist practices, joins the ethical and the epistemological by asking about the practical consequences of a theological symbol and by formulating norms of emancipatory praxis for revisioning Christian symbols. As "saving" work, feminist theology is itself a type of ethical and moral practice aimed at survival and flourishing. As such, its very nature is to produce discourses of emancipation that are self-conscious and reflective of their own cultural-political location and, as far as possible, of their emancipatory potential.

By way of summarily identifying the contours of theology as a practice within feminist liberationist Christianity, we can identify five specific characteristics. First, feminist theology is identified as a practice by the material norm of saving work. This norm of saving work signifies the promise and reality of Christianity, that God and God's people are involved in the saving work of the earth and all of its creatures. Saving work also signifies the critical and constructive activity of theology as ways of criticizing systems of distortion and dysfunction as well as ways of anticipating new possibilities. As such, saving work reminds us that the culture, our lives, our earth is in need of change and transformation: persons, creatures, and the earth are groaning in travail. Such suffering includes individual lives, interpersonal social systems, and ecological realities.

Second, theology as a practice of saving work brings together ethics and epistemology within both its communal and personal dimensions. For theology to be a form of knowledge as a practice, as we have seen, persons and communities engaged in theology must be shaped in virtues, must learn to know from action even as they learn to act. Third, ethics and epistemology are closely linked also to ideology critique, the critical analysis of relations of knowledge, power, and interest in society and how that affects social structures, cultural representations, forms of subjectivity, and the structuring of interpersonal relations. Theology as a practice is a critical theory, in the words of Raymond Geuss, "a reflective theory inherently productive of enlightenment and emancipation."[21]

Knowledge in feminist theology also involves, fourth, the anticipation of future possibilities. As we face the crises of knowledge, power, and values, knowledge of God and world requires a new aesthetic funding, a way of knowledge that is productive of new forms of survival and flourishing. To do this, aesthetics plays an important role in the language of theology. Attention to aesthetics in the practice of theology aids in the creation of new symbols, new meanings, and new narratives of Christian practice.[22]

Finally, theology as a practice may be identified by its contextuality. The notion of all theology as local is a popular one, with quite specific meanings for feminist theology.[23] As we have seen, feminist theology is contextual in that it helps persons to interpret, to analyze, and to transform their worlds. It helps women and men to have the power to speak; it is contextual as it works through the sufferings and desires of persons. Theology is thus contextual in terms of particular cultural situations, including speaking in and through such situations to broader global realities. But theology as a practice, situated within a particular context, also requires a reflexive awareness of its own limits, or as Charles Peirce described it, its own fallibilism. The point is not to offer the final truth, the correct interpretation of Christianity, or even correlations between cultural meanings and Christian interpretations. Rather, the point of feminist theology is to be open to correction and change and to do what we can to contribute to saving work.

Symbolic Patterning
and Saving Work

Feminist theology, as engaged in emancipatory praxis, recon-structs the symbolic patterns of Christianity. I have already alluded to this through the symbolic interpretations of patriarchy as sin and of communal spaces of transformation as grace. Examples of femi-nist symbolic patterning are numerous. Rita Nakashima Brock takes the symbol of Christology and addresses the healing of wounded-ness of women and men via the reconstruction of Christ and com-munity.[24] Jacquelyn Grant compares the Christologies of white women and black women, displaying the racism in many of the white women's Christologies.[25] Rosemary Radford Ruether's *Sexism and God-Talk* attempts to reconstruct Christian symbols and doc-trines through a critique of patriarchy and a focus on experiences of women.[26] The symbols are used to critique patriarchy, to both create and express the narratives of women and of men and to envision so-cial, planetary transformation. Indeed some of the richest and most vital reconstruction of symbols occurs in feminist theology because in a very real sense these symbols are already present in the praxis of feminist liberationist Christianity.

Symbols, like the representation of beliefs and actions, are open to interpretation and transformation. Just as they have no one way of working in the history of Christianity, so now are they open to change and possibility. They interact with the experience, struggles, hope, and faith of present Christians. The theologian, to use the term invoked in the introduction to this chapter, is as much a quilter as a hermeneutician. In one sense the symbols are given, but in another sense, because of the nature of symbols, they are open to change and transformation.

The specificity of feminist systematic theology, as I have already suggested, can be understood under the notion of saving work. Un-like theologies such as Tillich's that begin with a definition of reli-gion as ultimate concern, feminist theology begins simply with a reading of Christianity: Christian theology is about saving work. By this I mean that it is the work of feminist theologians to produce and create discourse (what all thinkers do, even when they say they are only interpreting), through the ongoing envisioning of Christian symbols. What links and interrelates these symbols and their constructions is the quest for emancipation, the belief that this is the goal, activity, and being of God in the world, that this is the movement of Christian praxis and the nature of Christian community. This does not mean, of course, that emancipatory praxis is a blueprint of a particular way of life; rather, as already suggested, it is an envisionment of new spaces for planetary and human flourishing. Pragmatic in intent, it addresses particular problems, from ecological disaster to harmful liturgy, to the nature of language as fluid and constitutive rather than static and representative. Feminist theology works to create emancipatory praxis. Three meanings can be imparted from this notion: (1) theology works, or functions, within the emancipatory praxis of feminist liberationist Christianity; (2) theology states what the envisionment of new symbols mean—pointing always to how symbols themselves work to break through the past and envision transformation[27]; and, (3) theology as emancipatory praxis is itself transformative. Feminist theology is performative and productive rather than merely descriptive, interpretive, or explanatory. Women and men engaged in feminist practices of theological education use feminist theology to persuade, to change, to open up, and to transform.

Theology, then, provides a symbolic content of faith. This symbolic content relates to how we interpret the world, how we experience the world in our spirituality, and how we work for change and transformation. Based within feminist theology, we can say that theology is a refashioning of doctrines that involves a symbolic patterning, a naming of Christian piety, and a kind of strategic employment of transforming praxis. These three activities are connected and interdependent. In symbolic patterning there is an interrelationship among doctrines and symbols that creates in narrative form an interpretive framework that serves to constitute Christian experience. Thus the symbolic patterning of Christian theology cannot be separated from the spirituality or piety it supports (and also articulates). Theology thus names piety, in the sense of supporting and articulating it, in different ways and on different levels. The naming of piety includes the formation of spiritual practices, the work of community, and respectful relationship with creation. And finally, theology's symbolic patterning and its naming of piety enable the Christian community to envision and then transform its life together and its life in the world. That systematic theology involves such an employment of transforming praxis is newly emphasized in feminist theology, as women and men attempt to use the polyvalence of symbols to envision both communal and personal transformation.

By polyvalence of the symbol I mean that, for instance, the symbol of God—the symbol of the ultimate, the perfection, the depth—has many functions and meanings. "God" works to tie other symbols (Christ, the church, scripture) together and functions to give religious values ultimate meaning. God can mean, in the Christian tradition, that we are loved unconditionally, that we experience ultimacy in terms of judgment, or anxiety, or the longing of love. Indeed, in Christian traditions the very mystery of God signifies the inexhaustible possibilities of meaning. As Elizabeth Johnson has observed,

> Speech about God shapes the life orientation not only of the corporate faith community but in this matrix guides its individual members as well. . . . The symbol of God functions. Neither abstract in content nor neutral in its effect, speaking about God sums up, unifies, and expresses a faith community's sense of ultimate mystery, the world view and expectation or order devolving from this, and the concomitant orientation of human life and devotion.[28]

Feminist theologians speak of God. I want to sketch how feminists speak of God in order to explore the task of deconstructing patriarchal meanings and functions of God symbols, the task of constructing new meanings and functions of God symbols, and the task of transforming reality in relation to new God symbols. It has been my experience that the three tasks of deconstruction, reconstruction, and transformation occur simultaneously for many, with different women starting at different points. For some, the deconstruction of an intensely patriarchal God is necessary to create space for life, let alone faith. For other women and men the imaginative reconstruction of God symbols moves them to deconstructing patriarchal meanings and functions of God symbols, while for still others it is the power of the symbol of God in the revisioning of the social order (or of Christianity) that leads them to both critique patriarchal notions and to fashion new symbols of God. Different feminists focus on different dimensions of Christian praxis at different points. For some, spirituality calls forth their feminist construct of symbols; for others, the nature of community draws their creative envisionment. But I will, by way of imposing a type of clarity, begin with the task of deconstructing, and in each of the tasks blend together both feminist works within Christianity and within the social order.

Deconstructing Patriarchal Meanings and Functions of God Symbols

The critique of Christian concepts of God lies first in its identification with "maleness" and the assumption and practice that women cannot represent God because they are not male. Mary Daly's riveting *Beyond God the Father* still wins wide acceptance in her dictum, "If God is male, then the male is God."[29] This identification of God as male has had innumerable destructive effects. In the Christian community the identification of God as male has resulted, time and time again, in the denial of leadership positions to women. The maleness of God has meant that women were not permitted to become theologians, and in some churches, not even allowed to teach boys and men. Thus God as male has to be criticized for a kind of idolatry, as Marcia Falk has noted, an idolatry within the church of elevating the power of men over women.[30]

If the symbol of God as male has functioned within the church to create a two-caste system, in the spirituality of women it has led to narratives that too often create selves with little dignity or respect. This image of the maleness of God is filled in with values of judgment without love, of distance and transcendence without intimacy and immanence. As Carter Heyward observed, many of the central images of God in theology deny or displace God's relatedness to the earth, images such as "being itself" or "wholly other."[31] At its worst, as Susan Brooks Thistlethwaite has observed, patriarchal images contribute to abuse of women and to women's acceptance of such abuse.[32] To deconstruct patriarchal images of God is to question the value of self-denial.

Feminists have done a great deal of work on the function and meaning of God symbols in the broader social order. Analysis of how symbols of "God" function in the broader social order includes arguments about how values, especially ultimate values, get assigned, and how values get represented in particular images and myths. Sallie McFague has analyzed how the image of "God as king" has functioned to represent in the broader social order the activity of domination.[33] I have, in *The Power to Speak*, been concerned with how a kind of "monotheistic" ordering gets established in society, in which patriarchy becomes the substitute for God and values and places in life get assigned by a so-called "natural" ordering.[34]

In summary, one of the primary tasks of feminist theology is to deconstruct patriarchal images of God. Such deconstruction occurs through a study of the effects (how the symbol has functioned), through arguments about the ability of the symbol to operate in polyvalent ways, and through the internal critique of Christian traditions of representation. In its critiques of how God has been symbolized and how the idea of God has functioned in Christianity and in the broader social order, feminist theology resists patriarchy as a comprehensive system of personal and political oppression, including the ongoing mutation of patriarchy through large veins and small capillaries of power.

Constructing New Meanings and Functions of God Symbols

Within this critique, feminists speak boldly to create new meanings and functions for the symbol "God." As Marjorie Procter-Smith said, "Our imaginations have been colonized by patriarchal culture."[35] Indeed, a great deal of feminist literature, which explores this theme over and over again, is invoked to identify God within various experiences of women and to define women's lives in and through God. "After a long season of thirst," Elizabeth Johnson noted, there is no reason not to respect the ways and forms in which women carry the *imago dei*. Women carry the image in many ways and thus carry also the responsibilities the *imago dei* entails.[36]

And with this notion of God comes new narratives of Christian life—a life lived in relation, in practical experiences. If patriarchal Christianity has ordered the meaning and structure of life through a hierarchy of divisions in which everyone and everything has its place, the feminist vision of life as relatedness is more fluid, more connected. Relationality is imaged as a web. Sally Purvis captures this deep sense of feminist spirituality:

> The shape and strength and even ongoing existence of a web depends on the strong bonds between each of the strands. Furthermore, each part of the web contributes to and is dependent on the strength of every other part, not just those strands that are the closest. It is in the best interest of each part to strengthen every other part; survival depends on cooperation, not competition. A strain on any part will reverberate through the whole. Each part has its being only as part of the whole.[37]

Many feminists identify their theologies as liberating or prophetic theologies, with a clear intent to understand the social order from a point of view of liberation. In these theological practices, the images of God are drawn from within liberating and prophetic traditions within Christianity to be critical of the social order, which is filled with oppression and idolatry. Images of God such as "wisdom" and "the mother" lift to ultimacy of value dimensions of care, practicality, and new birth.[38]

The revisioning of the symbol "God," in feminist theology, contains the emphasis on diverse ways of hearing God and seeing God. It is odd that in a religious tradition that stresses the many attributes of God and the mystery of God, theologians so often want to stress one fundamental form of speaking of God or of experiencing God. In feminist theology, the recognition of a multiplicity of ways of speaking of God is tied to the diversity of human beings. Take, for instance, Jacqueline Grant's comparison of three white women's discourses on Jesus in relation to black womanist discourse. While Grant shows how white women's Christologies can and should be viewed as different when related to one another, when related to black women's theologies, white women's Christologies share a common racism.[39] To speak of the experience of God is to discover and explore the experience and discourse different persons experience, and how they relate, in ambiguity and complexity to each other.

Transforming Reality in Relation to New Symbols of God

A third task of theology is the envisionment of transformation, the development of new ways of being and doing. Because patriarchy has been so fundamental to how we experience and structure the world, feminist theology must necessarily begin to transform the structures, images, and patterns of symbols about being human. In the area of spirituality, writers such as Carter Heyward and Rita Nakashima Brock have focused on the notion of eros and the transformation of the very process of spirituality. The erotic names the possibility of spiritual relations with the world through embodiment, connection, and justice.[40]

Though connectedness names the nature and presence of relations, it is what Brock calls eros that identifies that this connection is one of movement, passion, and transformation. To invoke the language of human love and even sexuality is not new in Christian theology—as traditional a writer as Augustine often writes in charged erotic tones.

In community the ekklesia is transformed through new processes, new liturgies, and new practices. Rosemary Radford Ruether's *Women-Church* contributes new liturgies, such as a rite of healing from violence, a rite of healing for an incest victim, a rite of healing for a victim of wife beating, and a puberty rite for a young woman.[41] Elisabeth Schüssler Fiorenza envisions the ideal of women-church as a democratic community, with men and women engaged in their own self-determination.[42] Though some may see this in the change of the institutional church, others envision a new church, a church with different forms, structures, and practices.

In the social and natural world, feminist ecological theologians have blended together ecological theology with feminism, creating an eco-feminist theology that reorders the relations between humans and the earth even as it reimages the earth as God's body, as the human home. Sallie McFague, in *The Body of God*, suggests that the body of God is "not a body, but all the different, peculiar, particular bodies about us."[43] Envisioning the body of God, world, and oneself together encourages a new ecological ethic, one that dares us to love all bodies more.

Rhetorical Strategies/Contextual Norms

But what can guide this work with symbols? How do women engaged in feminist practices of theological education know when to create new meanings and functions of God symbols, critique patriarchal orderings, and shape transforming visions? What methods guide this practice and what authorities govern theological activity?

In a practice of theology in which understanding is fashioned after the model of *transformation*, some notion of rhetoric will cover the procedures and methods of that theology. Rhetoric is, of course, the art of deliberation, persuasion, and judgment. It is the art of determining that which can be other, in a classical sense. Especially in the Roman tradition, the tradition that has most influenced thinkers such as Augustine and Calvin, rhetoric is that form of understanding which is aimed at action.[44] In this tradition, as Don Compier suggests, textual inquiry serves action and not vice versa.[45]

Rhetoric judges what it is that ought to be done and thus requires attention to the relations of power, agency, and structure in a particular situation. Well suited to the contextuality of knowledge, rhetoric is also sensitive to moral persuasion within the community and in the larger pluralistic setting. Attentiveness to strategies of rhetoric allow theologians to meet their fundamental religious and theoretical goal: the persuasion to emancipatory praxis.

Philosophically, when pluralism is acknowledged and sure foundations cease to be sought after, rhetoric emerges as the way of deliberation. Rather than putting aside the struggles and dreams, the beliefs and practices involved in a particular situation, persons use these to explore common ground, to discover imaginative possibilities, to find new solutions, and to create new forms of life. Likewise, once the political construction of knowledge is accepted, rhetoric becomes the basis of self-conscious deliberation and transformation. In Terry Eagleton's words, "Rhetoric, in other words, precedes logic: grasping propositions is only possible in specific forms of social life."[46]

Rhetorical forms of argument attempt to name what is going on, to reveal distortion and corruption, to imagine possibilities out of present reality. The norms used in rhetorical argument will themselves be taken from the situation; that is, they will be material as compared to transcendental norms. As Marilyn Hawkesworth observes, feminist rhetorical strategies "call worlds into being, inscribe new orders of possibilities, validate frames of reference, accredit forms of explanation, and reconstitute history as serviceable for present and future projects."[47]

Elisabeth Schüssler Fiorenza suggests that rhetoric is the metaphor for argument when quilting is the vision of the theological task.[48] She lists four rhetorical strategies found in the *ekklesia:* rhetorics of liberation, rhetorics of differences, rhetorics of equality, and rhetorics of vision.[49] The *rhetorics of liberation* is the critique of patriarchy, especially the false consciousness that can "naturalize, theologize, and mystify kyriarchal relations of subordination, exploitation, and oppression."[50] The *rhetorics of differences* reads biblical texts from different subject locations; the *rhetorics of equality* considers biblical truth through the democratic vision of the *basiliea.* The *rhetorics of vision* utilizes biblical texts for religious visions "that foster equality, justice, and the logic of the *ekklesia* rather than that of patriarchal domination."[51] Similarly, in redefining beauty, feminist theology "reorders values, norms, and meanings," as Megan Beverly has said.[52]

Women and men in feminist practices of theological education engage in the tasks of the critique of patriarchy, the naming of women's experience, and the construction of Christianity and culture, and they employ a wide variety of rhetorical strategies. Some of them are subversive, attempting to provide within the pluralism of forms of Christian symbols a critique of oppression and a vision. Some are strategies of resistance: a refusal to accept part of the tradition as tradition and to be willing to renounce as unretrievable part of the tradition. Some rhetorical strategies are loyal and friendly, as when a text such as *She Who Is* by Elizabeth Johnson finds the tradition fundamentally open to her feminist visions. Still other strategies empower women to claim their activity as theologians, as imaginative quilters of Christianity. The strategies are tools for the work; the performance and the product are the actual work of theology. As compared to models of theology in which explanation is the way of understanding and methods become themselves the focus of theology, in this model transformation as a way of understanding requires the methods to always serve the saving activity of theology.

Women and men in feminist practices of theological education learn the art of rhetoric. The norms for this art are found in the authority of practical possibilities in the future. Norms of the work of theology as saving activity require methods based on answers to the following questions:

Who is speaking and from what location?
Whose purpose does the discourse serve?
What vision is produced through the practical possibilities?
In what way is this vision one of great social, personal, and
    planetary flourishing?

The norms and authorities have to do with saving activity of the present toward the future. Such norms are neither universal nor from the tradition, because such norms may simply be illusions and too dangerous to the survival of the "others" of history. Universal norms, at least in recent history, serve the interest of those whose lives they represent, in many cases white Eurocentric men. And the norms of the tradition may well also be inscribed with patriarchy and sin. In fact, since hermeneutics does play a role in theology, it is always a present interpretation we have of the past, and any interpretation may well be distorted and corrupted. Intellectual honesty forces us to view the norms in front of us as themselves always subject to debate. Survival—personal, social, and planetary—begs us to not let our norms and authorities be subsumed too quickly under customary habits and unreflective activity.

Conclusion

That narrativity and ecclesiology are practices central to education is no surprise. And, for theological education, some concept of theology as naming the very nature of specifically *theological* education is necessary. Feminist theologies that attempt a quite new way to envision "theology" also share with the works of Edward Farley, David Kelsey, and others a commitment to find new ways to envision and construct theology.

Feminist practices of theology in theological education quite intently focus theology around the notion of what I have called "saving work." Saving work is oriented to the present and the future and combines a productive or rhetorical stress with a hermeneutical one. Theology, in the rubric of saving work, is not just about interpreting texts, but also about producing discourses of emancipation. Because the saving work of theology is concerned with ideas, not in an abstract sense, but in terms of their function or concrete use, attentiveness to cultural and political constructs shapes the construction and interpretation of feminist theology.

This chapter has sought to build upon the previous chapters to begin to explore feminist practices of theological education as not only a product in which students are required to demonstrate mastery (or to say it more actively, in which they are inseminated) but a process and activity in which students, and faculty, engage. In feminist practices of theology, students learn by doing the saving work of theology: revisioning God away from patriarchal destruction, considering how symbols actually work in their churches, and envisioning new ways of flourishing. In this feminist practice of theology, the themes of dialogue, justice, and imagination are again present.

Dialogue is necessary in the ongoing interpretation of texts as well as in situations, especially in terms of how ideas function in situations. As we saw in the comparison of feminist theology with other models of theology, dialogue can take a variety of forms in feminist theology: the deconstructive, the hermeneutical, and the cultural-linguistic. Like the deconstructive model, dialogue in feminist theology seeks to reveal and oppose the ordering and production of meaning through binary opposition. Yet dialogue in feminist theology carries a sort of critical excess beyond the "deconstruction" operative in the theological model of deconstruction. For feminist theology, deconstruction includes the subversiveness of how nondominant groups were able to read texts and use symbols differently.

Feminist theological practices also share a sense of dialogue with hermeneutical theologies, since dialogue stresses both the continual act of interpretation and the ongoing revisioning of "tradition" as itself a truly Christian act. Yet the theme of dialogue in feminist theology is combined with the theme of justice to focus interpretation on the rhetorical and contextual norms of saving work. And because feminist theology tends to emphasize the "risk" and "reconstructive" aspect of all interpretation in a far stronger sense than hermeneutical theologies, the theme of imagination is intertwined with that of dialogue and justice. This intertwining of justice, dialogue, and imagination also distinguishes feminist theology from the cultural-linguistic model, though feminist theology shares with this model the stress on how symbols and ideas function as a kind of grammar of faith.

The theme of dialogue becomes strongly combined with a theme of justice in the activity of feminist theology. Central to theology as saving work is the presence of justice as a theme in theological education. This theme emerges in the interpretation of texts and situations around issues of oppression and destruction, and in empowering diverse voices to speak, and in constructing new symbols of and for flourishing. In this way, justice is not merely a product but a process of bringing the ethical and the moral to bear upon the process of learning itself.

Finally, the theme of imagination is present in the feminist practice of theology as saving work. Aimed at emancipation that is transformative, feminist theology accepts the necessity of imaginatively constructing new meanings for symbols, new ways of flourishing, new discourses of emancipatory praxis. Feminist theological practices open themselves to poetry and prose as well as analysis and critique since theology is a saving work aimed at the present and the future. The very genre of feminist theology is opened up to include poetic texts on imagining God (or other symbols), autobiographical texts, and cultural-political analysis texts on the function of ideas in historical situations.

The theme of imagination means that the *process* of theological construction as well as the *product* of theological construction include a variety of approaches and styles. Megan Beverly's words name the process and product of theology as symbolized in the crazy quilt:

A crazy quilt is made from hundreds of scraps of material of all different sizes, textures, colors, and shapes. It is beautiful in its diversity. . . . The crazy quilt represents what Christian feminist theology is about. The quilt itself represents the piecing together of our everyday experience in a communal act of love and the acceptance of all people and life experiences. It redefines beauty, and by redefining what is beautiful, feminist theology deconstructs and reorders values, norms, and structures.[53]

5. *A Particular Vision: New Ways of Thinking about Theological Education*

It is time to evaluate my argument concerning feminist practices of theological education. I began this book with a wager that in order to address the specificity of feminist practices of theological education I would need to detour from the present conversation on theological education, which concentrates on the ideal aim of theological studies. Because, at least thus far, the current conversation about theological education has not focused on the students (who, quite literally, are the subjects of theological education), the social context in which students act, or the symbolic realm of Christian faith, I have had to focus on feminist *practices* of theological education.

The pragmatic method in this book parallels the method of feminist theology. Like all pragmatic methods, the one developed throughout this book is one of examining how ideas function in the context of human action. And, just as with many attempts at inquiry into relatively "uncharted" territory, this one has led me not to final answers, but to a working hypothesis about the need to speak from and within one movement around specific practices at work, and how those specific practices are named through feminist theological construction.

In the conventional model of how ideas influence actions, ideas supply the ultimate values to which ends are shaped.[1] In this conventional model, commitment to the idea is the reigning regulative and motivational fact. In my alternative model, ideas, values, and actions all shape one another, but not in any unchanging pattern. Rather, values, actions, and ideas all exist within practices and operate to address particular problems or issues. I am suggesting that within theological education, it is the practices that now have in some sense the "prior" reality, around which we understand and construct the ideas. Ideas both reflect and guide practices. Any discussion of theological ideas must consider not only the ideas in themselves but how they are used, what they are used for, and what range of activities and meanings they allow within a practice. The focus of this book has been to construct the ideas of feminist theology within the practices of feminist theological education. Feminist theology, at least as it is produced and used in theological education, works to represent, critique, and guide certain practices of theological education.

In a fallible and tentative way, I want to summarize the ideas and values within the feminist practices considered in this text. This summary serves not only to portray my argument in some comprehensive fashion but also to determine what the argument means about "education" viewed from within feminism, and what implications it might hold for a new type of conversation about the present status of theological education. My argument in this chapter has four steps: first, a partial vision of education as a summary of the practices considered in the body of this text; second, a view of education as process within this feminist vision; third, a redefinition of our way of thinking about theological education beyond mere curriculum reform; and fourth, in conclusion, a warning of realism to women engaged in the practices of feminist theological education.

By way of summary, all I offer is a particular vision of feminist theological education. By particular vision I mean that any feminist vision drawn from the practices that we have charted is particular in the sense that it arises from these practices and also in the sense that it is my particular vision, that which I see. The term *particular* thus refers both to the concreteness and specificity of feminist practices and to the fact that, the moment one interprets such practices, the concreteness and specificity of the interpretation is formed through the writer's own perspectives and commitments. *Particular* has one more meaning that I want to draw on, and that is its use in logic, where it designates a proposition that affirms or denies a predicate to a part of the subject; that is, particular as meaning nonuniversal. This particular vision is not universal to the whole of theology, and it is precisely the *particularity* of the vision that can open up new ways to discuss theological education. I participate in feminist practices of theological education with my particular limits, resources, and perspectives. Hans-Georg Gadamer has suggested that such prejudgments are our access points to broader horizons of understanding. I will try to make this so, but where I err, the reader is encouraged to differ from my vision boldly!

This particular vision arises at least in part because feminist practices of theological education, like feminism in general, can be explained neither as a correction to a Christian essence in terms of demanding equal rights nor as a supplementation to a Christian essence by lifting up the special gifts of women. As we have already seen, feminist Christianity represents a new type of Christianity, one which requires its own terms of understanding. Different forms of Christianity take on different emphases and shapes of piety and prayer, of worship and service, of education and morality, and of understanding and language. The pietist movement emphasized that heart-felt experience required a theological understanding of the subjectivity of feeling and intention, a well-developed discourse of the heart, so to speak. The language of real presence in medieval Christianity makes sense when one understands the liturgical and aesthetic practices of that time. Contemporary feminist Christianity requires understanding within its own practices.[2]

It is only by standing within feminist liberationist Christianity that a particular vision emerges from the blending or perhaps weaving of all three practices in order to disclose the values, purposes, and themes that constitute the internal goods of the practices of feminist theological education. This weaving can occur through a recollection of the practices we have covered. The activity of recollection is not a mere literal remembering but a collecting together again in new ways that may well enable new understandings and visions of theological education.

The first practice considered was that of narrativity, the writing of one's life. It is not a static story, nor a set plot; rather, narrativity stresses the ongoing activity of writing one's life. Christianity has always included the practice of narrativity. In settled times this activity may entail appropriating fairly fixed narratives, while in times of great change this activity may involve crafting quite new narratives. Narrativity, in most Christian forms, is surrounded by the ecclesia; in communion and community in reflection and working together, the Christian life is constantly written. There are, of course, many forms of narratives, and each narrative has its own distinctiveness, if not its own uniqueness. As with the narratives we read in books or see in films, different meanings can be attached and different interpretations offered. Yet the meanings and interpretations are always set in context of the narrative itself. Women are writing new narratives because they must.

Within these narratives certain ideas appear and reappear in various ways. Ideas of the subject as active agent, ideas of creativity and religious symbols, ideas of understanding and naming experiences in new ways are woven through these narratives. Values emerge: the privileging of difference; the revelation of the connectedness we have and the task of nurturing these connections; the respect of embodiment and the recognition that theology too is always embodied; and the valuing of friendship as a naming and vision of ultimacy.

It is these values that become the internal goods of the practice of narrativity. Women and men engaged in the practice of narrativity value connections, embodiment, creativity, and difference. It is important to understand that these values become ways of interpreting the world. Take the value of difference: engaged in feminist practices of theological education, women learn in various ways how to hear and appreciate difference. This may come through the sharing of a variety of stories, through open conflict, through enlarging knowledge about what goes on for different women around the world. If patriarchy creates and constructs some notion of essential identity, feminism deconstructs this universal category and replaces it with difference and specificity. This is not a matter simply of learning to see difference, but also of valuing and appreciating difference.

Another example might be that of connectedness. A woman engaged in practices of theological education will form her narrativity around connections to others, to God, to the world, as well as to the self. This connectedness will occur in rituals of community, in the emphasis on friendship, in classroom explorations of connectedness, and in social work for justice. The connectedness will be formed in women through images of God not as wholly disconnected other, but as a friend who is already connected. The idea of connectedness in feminist theology may shape the habits of one's daily life to use public transportation, to recycle, to spend time with friends in rest and recreation. The dual ideas of God as friend and of the earth as our home reinforce our solidarity with all and move our action toward greater flourishing. As a lens through which we understand reality, connectedness will be valued for its own intrinsic satisfaction. Women and men will learn the arts of nurturing connection, and the many ways that connections become distorted and broken.

Feminist theology works to provide tools for constructing new narratives for women and for clearing discursive spaces for women to enact their ongoing narrativity. That women must rewrite their lives in new ways must be understood as arising directly within the context of cultural patterns of change. Women, as I have already mentioned, lack narratives of themselves in theological education as well as in culture. Feminist theology provides important symbolic frames and values as resources to do this saving work. Yet, as we have seen, there are some preferred dimensions of narrativity represented in feminist theology: the valuing of contextuality, the privileging of difference, the naming of women's experiences, and the concern for moral agency. In feminist theology, symbols function in a quite practical way to enable the feminist practice of narrativity in theological education.

The practice of ekklesiality incorporates and expands many of the ideas in the practice of narrativity. Women and men engage in a variety of ekklesial practices, from struggles with ordination in established denominations, to development of alternative forms of community, to creation of feminist liturgies, to participation in spirituality groups. Feminist ecclesiology finds its spaces in a wide variety of places. Feminist ecclesiology, as we have seen, can be named symbolically in the denunciation of sin and the annunciation of grace.

The use of symbols such as sin and grace have allowed us to examine how it is that feminist theology constructs the ekklesia. The church as space for the denunciation of sin and annunciation of grace functions sacramentally as a visible sign of God's invisible grace. In invoking these symbols from the tradition, feminist theology also reworks the symbols in order to help women and men resist patriarchy and to shape new forms of flourishing. The ekklesia, for women and men, exists as the counter-public of justice, the community of friends, and the spirituality of connectedness.

Ideas of justice, connectedness, embodiment, and openness, represented in these symbols, are the internal goods of the practice of the ekklesia. Within the church, as within the world, justice is a necessary though not sufficient condition of friendship. Connectedness runs through both friendship and justice, for the connectedness of justice is the possibility that each may determine her or his own life and have a say in determining life together. The internal goods in the practice of ecclesiology are themselves connected and parallel to those of narrativity: values of mutuality and friendship, connectedness and embodiment, concreteness and transformation.

Once again, then, we can understand the saving work of feminist theology as expressing, criticizing, and guiding the practice of ekklesia. It is important to note that feminist theology provides an understanding of ekklesia within the broader context of the culture. The ekklesia, as sacrament, represents redemptive community to the world. And the very understanding of sin and grace symbolizes not only an understanding of church but also an understanding of culture. Indeed, ideas function within ecclesiology not so much to demarcate separate spaces of church and world, but to exemplify and express ongoing relations of ekklesia and world.

The critical and creative work of theology is itself a practice within feminist liberationist Christianity. Envisioned by one student as a "crazy quilt," feminist theology works to critically resist oppression and dehumanization and to construct ideas, symbols, and other resources for survival and human flourishing. As a type of understanding, feminist theology arises out of emancipatory praxis.[3] Joining the ethical and the epistemological, feminist theory is a pragmatic critical theory.

Central to the saving work of feminist theology as a pragmatic critical theory is symbolic construction. The symbolic construction of feminist theology works to emancipate from oppression and sin, to envision new spaces of flourishing, and to produce new ways of being in the world. Feminist theology deconstructs oppressive symbols and oppressive functions of symbols of God. Exploring different experiences of God and world, feminist theology opens up new meanings and functions through the symbol of God. Feminist theology works to envision transformation through new symbols of God and to develop discourses of God that are themselves transformative.

As with the practices of narrativity and ekklesiality, certain ideas and values are expressed. Theology envisions a God, as well as a church and a subject, that is fundamentally known through connections, mutuality, and friendship. Openness and the desire to appreciate difference name a fundamental perspective of theology's work. Justice is itself the binding quality of theology's own internal relations between ethics and epistemology.

Theology is saving work, and as such it is aimed at saving the present and finding new possibilities for the future. The idea of feminist theology as a practice can be best understood through rhetoric as a type of understanding aimed at action. To fashion theology as rhetoric is to attend self-consciously to the practical effectiveness of ideas. Feminists fashion different rhetorical strategies to accomplish saving work.

Feminist theology offers a rather holistic vision of what actually goes on in theological education. Out of the practices of narrativity, ekklesia, and theology such a particular vision arises. It is based on new images, values, and relations. Just as other historic forms of Christianity have continued practices such as these and changed them in relation to form, function, and meaning, so also has feminism transformed practices of Christianity. These practices create a way of being in the world for Christianity and shape, as we have seen, the nature and import of theological education.

Educational Process
in Feminist Practices

The concentration on practices enables us to think about education in new ways. To identify practices as the sites of learning in theological education is to avoid some common "divisions" in thinking about education and to require the development of new language to name the process of education. In a way, it avoids some of the problems in our usual way of talking about education, and it also provides us with new ways of thinking about education as a process and not simply as a product.

In most contemporary views of theological education, the task of education is to provide the individual with some sense of ordered learning. The focus is on the transmission of ideas, or, to put it quite literally for a seminary context, on the insemination of ideas. Many curriculums and pedagogy follow this assumption: that one begins with foundational courses that provide introductory materials and one directs students up the ladder, so to speak, in more and more advanced mastery of the subject matter. Pedagogy is focused on, for it conveys the information and helps the individual student master and express such information.

Though recent work on theological education has deconstructed the foundationalism, individualism, and rationalism of modern ideas of education, the constructive suggestions usually return or remain limited to questions of how to order cognitive learning. Edward Farley, for instance, suggests the notion of *theologia* as a type of reflective wisdom, a suggestion quite close, as I have noted before, to feminist concerns for education as a whole process. But when Farley provides his own constructive hints at how to accomplish this process, his suggestions are about cognitive ordering. As Craig Dykstra has observed, Farley tends to limit the scope of his understanding of "cognition" to linguistic and logical-mathematical realms.[4] Howard Gardner, whom Dykstra cites, has identified seven kinds of intelligence, or what we might call ways of knowing: linguistic, musical, logical-mathematical, spatial, bodily-kinesthetic, and two personal forms (that might be called feeling and intuition).[5] While Farley's call for *theologia* invites an expanded vision of education beyond a new rearranging of "ordered" learning, his constructive suggestions, at least thus far, are limited to revisions of cognitive learning. The same type of criticism of unrealized potential can be made against David Kelsey's constructive suggestions in *To Understand God Truly*. Though Kelsey draws attention to practices, when he moves to issues of actual change and transformation in theological education, his concern is mainly with disciplines. And though he accepts Farley's aim of *habitus*, he argues that the way to achieve such reflective wisdom is to continue the types of critical thinking that have dominated modernity.[6]

The advantage of focusing on the practices of a specific movement within theological education is that it both requires and allows a fuller range of forms of knowing. To focus on practices shifts the educational gaze, so to speak, away from the gap between ideas and their applications and causes us to look at how persons are already engaged in a set of practices in and through which they are always constructing and organizing ideas. Feminist practices as social activities require us to be sensitive to "knowing" as an intersubjective and embodied process; knowing appeals to an anthropology that is both communal and physical.[7]

Feminist theorists of education have often pointed out that "knowing" for women has to be understood in terms of physical presence, relationships with students and faculty, and connections between feelings and ideas. The book *Women's Ways of Knowing* identifies the following kinds of knowledge: received, subjective (in terms of the inner voice and the quest for self), procedural (reason as well as separate and connected knowing), and constructed.[8] The authors suggest that dominant models of education hinder women's process of education because the educational models continue to be based on modern assumptions of epistemology. The text then offers some suggestions for reconceiving knowledge and education based on the actual practices of women. Likewise, Patricia Hill Collins in *Black Feminist Thought* develops what she calls an "Afrocentric feminist epistemology" based on the practices of concrete experience as a criterion of meaning, the use of dialogue in assessing knowledge claims, the ethic of caring, and an ethic of accountability.[9]

But developing new models of "knowing" is not unique to feminism. Historically, as David Kelsey has suggested, there are quite different forms of epistemology in relation to theology. Some of the contemporary theological models discussed in chapter 4 are concerned with developing new models of knowing, given the pluralism of culture and anti-foundationalism of contemporary epistemology. David Tracy and George Lindbeck use hermeneutical and linguistic theories to provide new understandings of "knowing" within what they call religious traditions. Susan Hekman, in *Gender and Knowledge,* relates complementary postmodern and feminist forms of epistemology.[10]

It has been the argument of this text that one of the distinctive characteristics of feminist practices is that they provide the resource for new forms of knowing and for new understandings of theological education. To focus on specific practices, as we have done in this text, allows us both to enlarge the nature of "knowing" beyond that utilized in modern theological education and to name some specific components of the education process in which this "knowing" is engaged. In the context of our investigation of feminist practices at least three themes emerge within each practice: imagination, dialogue, and justice.

Utilizing these themes, I want to move toward conceiving education as a process and not merely a product. I want to contend that feminist theology both requires and contributes a process of education that is a training in imagination, dialogue, and justice, even as it is an insemination of ideas from the past.

Justice

At the conclusion of *God's Fierce Whimsy,* the women of the Mud Flower Collective contend that "the fundamental goal of theological education must be the doing of justice."[11] Likewise, Elisabeth Schüssler Fiorenza places the doing of justice at the center of theological education:

> I have argued that theology and theological education must be conceived as a transformative discursive praxis that critically reflects on the concrete historical-political configurations and theological practices of Christian communities which have engendered and still engender the exclusion and dehumanization of "the others" of free born, educated and propertied men in Western society. At the same time it must seek to articulate alternative communal visions and values for the human community on the brink of atomic annihilation. Such a conception of theology cannot just limit itself to a critical reflection on religious and ecclesial practices. It is foremost a critical reflection on the social-cultural-political practices in which religious communities have been and still are embedded and to which they contribute.[12]

Justice, as a basic theme of theological education, is central to each practice of feminist theological education. In narrativity a communicative possibility of justice prevails: each person gets a voice in self-determination. The activity of writing one's life in relation to self, others, and earth is an act of being drawn out, learning to shape and be shaped in right relationship. In the practice of ekklesia the church as a counter-public of justice names a space in which ways of justice are modeled and formed. Justice, as we have seen, defines the nature and mission of the ekklesia. And in the feminist practice of theology, justice is central to the braiding together of ethics and epistemology in the formation of new meanings and functions of symbols and the development of new discursive practices.

Likewise, in terms of the questions of subject, culture, and symbol that I introduced in chapter 1, justice is an important theme. In contemporary theology, visions of justice are central to the new symbols and new meanings of symbols in theology. Justice as a key to symbolic life of Christianity is represented not only in feminist theology but also in African American, Latin American, and other forms of liberation theology. Within the various theologies of liberation movements, the symbolic construction of justice seeks to express the dialectical movement within the function of Christian symbols: justice enables us to name faith, and faith symbols reconceived as justice allow us to envision new spaces of life together.

One of the quests of this book has been to understand the broader cultural context of contemporary theological education. I have suggested that the very presence of women, in great diversity, represents many of the cultural struggles of the day. The struggle for justice in American culture and in the world is centrally involved in hearing voices that have been marginalized, but also envisioning new spaces in church and culture for the living out of justice. Thus justice demands, in a sense, the focus on particular human subjects, the participation of different voices, and the articulation of different concerns and needs.

But theological education is not just *about* justice, it is, in a sense, justice itself. We need to conceive of theological education as the doing of justice, with justice as a central theme, along with "ordered" learning, imaginative envisioning, and dialogue. In American history the parallel referent, and that which feminist theology continues, is the understanding of education as the training of citizens. Justice names not simply the goal but the process itself.

Sharon Welch has called for a contemporary sense of this same notion of education in her language of communicative ethics.[13]

Welch argues that justice can be central only with the material and discursive relations between different groups. And this communicative ethic, as a basic shape of the education process, is based on solidarity. Solidarity, according to Welch, includes both the granting of respect by different groups and, at the same time, recognition of the interdependency of different groups.

Dialogue

Thus justice, as a theme of education, is intertwined with solidarity, communication, and dialogue. Dialogue, within Welch's conception of communicative ethics, is not abstract dialogue. Welch is critical of Habermas and others who focus on the ideal of conversation, assuming that the "other" has simply been "excluded" from the conversation. Welch asks, "If the inclusion of women and minorities is simply a matter of extension, why has it been so long in coming?"[14] Dialogue requires real interaction among embodied persons, with openness and respect for mutual critique.

In theological education this material interaction might be envisioned by the creation of dialogical spaces. Theological education is a series of quite physical spaces: classrooms, hallways, and worship places, and sites of spirituality group and committee meetings. These physical spaces are filled with the bodies of students, faculty, and staff, representing many differences that have come to mark and define the present constitution of American Christianity and American culture.

The spaces of theological education, filled with persons who are different and seeking justice, are already "dialogical" places where lives meet, and where bodies interact on physical, emotional, and linguistic levels. In feminist theological education, these spaces are places where solidarity begins and where freedom occurs. As Maxine Greene has suggested, "We might think of freedom as an opening of spaces as well as perspectives."[15] Within feminist theological education, education is a dialogical process of concrete encounter with others enacted through classes, worship, committees. Education is about social interaction, and even reason within education is dialogical and communicative.[16]

Conversation has become a key term for the analysis of reading and writing texts. David Tracy suggests that reading a text is like having a genuine conversation and must be distinguished from idle chatter, debate, confrontation, and gossip.[17] Tracy's model of conversation, which he adapts from Hans-Georg Gadamer, is defined by letting the subject matter take over, by forgetting one's own self and letting understanding occur. Tracy understands true conversation as "letting the question take over." Tracy's conversation model provides us with a way of placing understanding as not merely getting the facts in, but in a "disclosive" fashion. Conversation entails risk, an engagement that we will be changed, and thus conversation also entails transformation.

As a kind of model for dialogue that is itself a process of conversation, Tracy's notion gives us key ingredients: understanding, risk, and transformation. Yet in relation to the theme of justice, Tracy's model needs to be challenged at an essential point: the emphasis on forgetting one's self. At least within feminist practices of theological education, true understanding occurs as the "concrete" self is affirmed and understood. Dialogue that attempts to abstract from concrete selves too often results in a privileging of a particular self who becomes the ideal model of conversation. Justice and the quest for emancipation require that dialogue is always among embodied and embedded selves who speak in their own voices and develop connections, including struggles and conflicts, within their actual context.[18] As Peter Hodgson has suggested, "Dialogue, while related to conceptual or logical rationality, is always pressing toward discursive or communicative practices that have freedom as their telos; thus the dialogical and the emancipatory are very closely related."[19]

Imagination

With the stress on material as well as discursive practices leading to transformation and the struggle and desire for new hope of justice, imagination is central to education. Imagination, the ability to think the new, is an act of survival. Yet the imagination is rarely explicit in the educational process and is usually relegated to a few small elective courses emphasizing how to use music in worship.

Feminist theology, as we have seen, makes imagination central, since the saving work of theology requires new imaginative visions. Indeed the very notion of a pragmatic critical theory requires imaginative reconstruction as well as analytical explanation. Central to feminist theological practice is recognizing the unrealized possibilities in a situation. Imagination, Iris Young tells us, "is the faculty of transforming the experience of what is into a projection of what could be, the faculty that frees thought to form ideals and norms."[20] And feminist ecclesiology is based on imagination in terms of envisioning the church in new spaces. Narrativity is also imaginative: the ability to imagine new possibilities for our lives and for the world.

Feminist theologies are replete with calls to the imagination, such as this from Marjorie Procter-Smith: "Anamnesis for women requires the creation of feminist imagination, which permits women to appropriate the past and to envision our future."[21] Elisabeth Schüssler Fiorenza has suggested that an important step in biblical hermeneutics and in theological education is the creative visualization of the text. Sallie McFague, Rita Nakashima Brock, and Rosemary Radford Ruether have all modeled what it is to imagine new symbols and new meanings for symbols of God.

Within feminist theology and feminist practices of theological education, this need and quest for reimagining means not only specific acts of reconstruction but also the inclusion of literature and poetry as sources of theological reflection. In many cases these *are* the written documents by women, and their use is central to the inclusion of "tradition" in feminist theology. But such prose and poetry not only represent what women wrote but also teach us an imaginative process of reconstructing women's lives, the church, and the very nature of reflection as aimed toward the future. Feminist theology includes poetic revisioning, aesthetic production, and imaginative construction.

It is ironic, in some ways, that modern theology and theological education have paid so little explicit attention to imagination and methods of imaginative revisioning. Modern theology, in thinkers such as Barth and Schleiermacher, Tillich and Rahner, and the Niebuhr brothers used imaginative revisioning to allow theology as the discourse of faith to survive the onslaught of modern rationality. Yet with the rare exception of thinkers such as Samuel Coleridge and Jonathan Edwards, the dimensions of imagination, beauty, and aesthetics were not emphasized as central to modern theological method.

In writings on theological education, imagination is usually confined to small appeals about the inclusion of the arts. One exception to this is Charles Wood's *Vision and Discernment*.[22] Wood is concerned with theology as critical inquiry into Christian witness. For Wood this is not simply about the present and past Christian witness but also about the future Christian witness. "As critical reflection upon the church's activity, theology is as much concerned with its prospective activity as with its history."[23] This prospective activity, within feminist practices of theological education, has to do with a form of knowing that envisions the future differently, that constructs new symbols of meaning, that provides us with the new patterns of action.

The role of imagination must not be seen to be some romantic turn in knowing in any negative sense. Indeed, contemporary epistemologies increasingly emphasize the metaphorical and aesthetic bases of all forms of knowing. To bring imagination as central into the educational process may well be one of the most crucial requirements of forming new ways of knowing and new ways of learning.

Redefining Our Way of Thinking about Theological Education

In this book I have tried to speak about feminist practices of theological education in part as a model of the kind of conversation that needs to occur in a second generation of conversation about theological education. I have attempted to offer what Fumitaka Matsuoka has identified as the future of discourse on theological education: "In a pluralistic and multicultural world the order of knowing and doing moves from particular to universal. In a multicultural world one becomes aware of one's own particularity, be it ethnicity, gender or class, with a recognition of one's dependence on the web of humankind."[24]

A basic argument of this text is that if we can direct our attention to actual practices of theological education in which students, faculty, and others participate, then we may begin to find ways of speaking about theological education as a process, as Maxine Greene called it, of "futuring" rather than simply a product of the insemination of ideas.[25] Indeed, what we need to do is to be reflective about "theological education" in terms of how the "theological" and the "educational" combine.

In feminist practices, as we have seen, the intertwining of the theological and the educational in specific practices means that rather than hold only to the narrow notion of "ordered learning" as the product of education, we can begin to experiment and explore a broader and more creative notion of education as process. I want to suggest that if we examine other practices of theological education, we can extend and enrich this view of education as a process, rather than a product. Central to my suggestion is the belief that change and transformation in theological education will never be achieved through curriculum reform alone. Rather, we must expand our discourse about theological education into the fuller range of educational process. Change and transformation will occur when we find new ways of envisioning the educational process through the network of actual and emergent practices within theological education. I suggest we begin to redefine our way of thinking of "theological education" in at least three significant ways.

First, theological education is about the relationships formed, the style of teaching, and the extracurricular activities as well as the curriculum. The question of pedagogical styles to encourage and train the imagination requires attention both because of emergent practices and because of the desire for change and transformation. Or, to take another example, the notion of all education as individually focused may need to be decentered (not necessarily replaced) with a notion of education as communal cooperative activity. There is an enormous range of practices, relationships, activities, and structures that are as important in theological education as is the curriculum. We need ways to speak of these from within particular movements and ways to speak on a more general network level.

Education may well be about "what we do" as well as "what we say." If theological education is about merely the ordered learning of cognitive ideas, then finding the right curriculum will solve all the current problems in theological education. But if knowing God is as much a matter of right relationships as it is a mastery of correct ideas, then the present crisis of theological education cannot be fixed merely by reordering the curriculum. New relationships of imagination, of justice, of dialogue must be formed in the midst of a pluralistic world and new forms of relating, teaching, and community building will have to be developed. The *how* of learning is directly related, in this notion of theological education as a process, to the *what* of learning. Indeed, the task for the subjects of theological education may be as much the doing of new forms of relationships to God, self, others, traditions, and society as it is the articulation of right ideas.

Second, theological education is formed in and through cultural problematics.[26] Education is a historical institution and, as such, always a representative and a participant in broader cultural trends. I have suggested that central to the conversation of theological education must be a discussion of current cultural problematics, such as the tremendous changes in women's lives, the problems of binary ordering and patriarchal oppression, and the role of intellectual

work as "saving" work. Furthermore, central to my focus on practices and theology within these practices is a foregrounding of cultural contexts within what and how we learn.

But in addition, a great many other "cultural" problematics or
issues must be addressed. Global concerns and concerns of racism,
multi-culturalism, and technology all must become the material
through which education thinks its future. To ignore or belittle these
cultural problematics in theological education is, to use the old
proverb, like trying to ignore the elephant standing in the middle of
the living room. These problematics are present in the lives of students, teachers, and staff. They represent the dominant questions
and possibilities for reflection and construction; they provide the
material through which learning can be about praxis, or reflective,
intentional living in Christian community.

In the tradition of pragmatist John Dewey, education is always a
"public" activity, concerned with providing persons resources for reflection on and transformation of the environment.[27] In feminist
practices, theology itself is about such "saving work." To learn to address the current issues of the day in light of the past, present, and
future reality of Christian praxis is to form education as a proces of
doing, rather than merely learning about, theology. And to take se-
riously the cultural problematics through which specific practices
are formulated is to begin to explore and identify connections between theological education and the local community from which
the students (and often faculty) come and to which they return.

Third, the symbolic patterns of religion and culture are inherently a part of theological education and need careful attention.
Thinking about theological education as a participation in the symbolic will include the construction and engagement in present and
future symbolic patterns as well as understanding and interpreting
symbolic thought in past centuries. Education is always engagement
in a symbolic environment. Students are taught the symbolic patterns of past centuries, and they should be taught how these symbols and ideas functioned within the practices of the time. But
students and teachers also need to engage in the symbolic struggles
of our day. Education, at least within a feminist vision, is about
forming persons to be symbolic constructors, about training persons
to be poets as well as interpreters.

One pressing issue of new envisioning of the symbolic patterning of Christianity is the concern for patterning that is open to bicultural and bilingual forms. As Christians in the United States learn
to live with many different voices and cultures, one of the greatest

needs in theological education will be to form persons in symbolic biculturalism, the ability to move and flourish amid various symbolic patterns. If students and faculty can learn how to read and anticipate the symbolic structures of their cultures, and to read and anticipate symbolic constructs in a bicultural fashion, theological education becomes formed as a process speaking to the needs of the day. To compare different cultures, past and present, in terms of how Christ, for instance, is imaged, functions, conceptualized, and so on, is to enter a kind of bicultural symbolic analysis.

By thinking about theological education as a process of the intertwining of theology and education in and through practices, within which different voices reflect and construct practices of theological education, we can arrive at some sense of how to move toward change and transformation in theological education. As I have indicated, change and transformation will be offered from new voices and new perspectives—new voices representing the pluralism within culture as a whole and within theological education, and new perspectives that allow us to speak about practices and utopian visions within these practices. Change and transformation occur, within this model, by tracing out the unrealized possibilities in the present.

The way forward, in my judgment, is a thick description of the present, including identifying emergent possibilities in the present. Clifford Geertz defines thick description as "an elaborate venture in" the "piled-up structures of inference and implication" in human events and structures.[28] To discuss change and transformation in theological education will be an elaborate venture of hearing different voices speak from their perspectives. Within all this speaking and hearing, creating thick descriptions of theological education will lead us not to an idea about ultimate aims (though that inference may also be included!) but to pile up structures of inference and implication within an intricate network of education as a process.

Conclusion: The Warning
and Hope of Utopian Realism

Throughout this book I have tried to identify what is special or unique in what women do in feminist practices of theological education and the vision of education (as well as Christianity) that arises out of these practices. I have consciously attempted to provide ways of naming what is among us, and far too often not seen, or is belittled, since it does not fit the dominant discourse about theological education.

But I would not be faithful to the women engaged in feminist practices of theological education if I did not end the book with a warning that this vision is still utopian, that it is the speaking of largely still *unrealized* possibilities in our midst even as it is expressed and constituted among us. Many feminist works have focused on the difficulties of women in theological education who engage in feminist practices (and those who don't consciously engage as well!).

In traveling around the United States and Canada researching this book, I was often struck by both the utopian hope and the factual realism that women expressed about the role of feminist practices within theological education. Women, and men, struggle to hold both the joyous hope of resistance and community together with the frustrating realism of continued oppression and belittlement in theological education. This struggle of hope and realism names, as well, my own experience as a woman in theological education. Very early on in my research, as I began to realize how my own struggles were repeated in countless times and ways, I read Gail Griffin's *Calling: Essays on Teaching in the Mother Tongue*, which identifies the struggles to deal with the feminist movement on a college campus.[29] One of the ways she symbolizes the complexities and paradoxes within the struggle is by the following story from *Alice in Wonderland.*

> The table was a large one, but the three were all crowded together at one corner of it. "No room, no room!" they cried out when they saw Alice coming. "There's plenty of room!" said Alice, indignantly, and she sat down in a large arm-chair at one end of the table.
>
> "Have some wine," the March Hare said, in an encouraging tone.
>
> Alice looked all round the table, but there was nothing on it but tea. "I don't see any wine," she remarked.
>
> "There isn't any," said the March Hare.
>
> "Then it wasn't very civil of you to offer it," said Alice, angrily.
>
> "It wasn't very civil of you to sit down without being invited," said the March Hare.
>
> "I didn't know it was your table," said Alice; "it's laid for a great many more than three."[30]

Women engaged in feminist practices come to the laden table of theological education ready to contribute, to feast, to talk, and to participate. Though the table, laden with the rich food of concepts, categories, symbols, practices, relationships, seems to invite women, they are often told that they haven't really been invited. There is still a dominant group and discourse that claims ownership of theological education, that adjudicates the discourse, that decides what is civil and what is rude, and that parcels out the riches of the table. Part of our struggle is that the table is abundant and inviting, but the March Hares tell us that despite appearances, we aren't invited.

But like Alice, we know that we *are already* at the table. The question is, how do we respond to the resources present in theological education, in the midst of all the mixed messages of beckoning and dismissal? In a chapter on theological education in her book *But She Said*, Elisabeth Schüssler Fiorenza contends that women not only have to move from lay to professional persona but from a "feminine supportive, marginal, silent, private *persona* to a masculine, assertive, central, speaking, public, one."[31] Women are supposed to master the discourses and disciplines of theological education and assume the subject position of an elite white Eurocentric male. Schüssler Fiorenza observes that women actually have three possibilities. The first possibility is that women can assume the masculine position and learn to do it like a man. The second possibility is that women can totally reject this subject position and try to find preferred "feminine" ways. This position usually refuses the resources within the academy, including the resources of changing the system. A third possibility is for women to become "bilingual" and learn the male system in order to transform it. Schüssler Fiorenza calls women who follow the third option *resident aliens*. A resident alien, Schüssler Fiorenza suggests, is both an insider and outsider, "insider by virtue of residence or patriarchal affiliation to a male citizen or institution; outsider in terms of language, experience, culture, and history."[32]

Certainly I advocate the third position. It is not easy, but neither are the other positions that Schüssler Fiorenza identifies. To deny what one has experienced and learned as a particular woman and try to act in ways that deny or contradict one's memories and desires is to become alienated from one's own history. To reject the structures in which we find ourselves, and all the resources on that abundant table, is to forgo the solidarity with the earth and with all those for whom the structures must change in order to secure survival, let alone flourish. But the position of a resident alien is difficult, for one never really is home, except where one can create even partial visions of a home with a table to which all are readily and eagerly invited.

Notes

Chapter 1: Women as Subjects
of Theological Education?

1. Rosemary Radford Ruether, *Sexism and God-Talk: Toward a Feminist Theology* (Boston: Beacon Press, 1983).
2. B. A. Gerrish, *Tradition and the Modern World: Reformed Theology in the Nineteenth Century* (Chicago and London: University of Chicago Press, 1978), 48.
3. William A. Clebsch, *From Sacred to Profane America: The Role of Religion in American History*, Classics in Religious Studies Series (Chico, Calif.: Scholars Press, 1968).
4. The Cornwall Collective, *Your Daughters Shall Prophesy: Feminist Alternatives in Theological Education* (New York: Pilgrim Press, 1980).
5. Ibid., 5.
6. The Mud Flower Collective, *God's Fierce Whimsy: Christian Feminism and Theological Education* (New York: Pilgrim Press, 1985), 3.
7. Ibid., 29–30.
8. Ibid., 27.
9. Edward Farley, *Theologia: The Fragmentation and Unity of Theological Education* (Philadelphia: Fortress Press, 1983).
10. Joseph C. Hough, Jr., and John B. Cobb, Jr., *Christian Identity and Theological Education* (Chico, Calif.: Scholars Press, 1985), 1. Emphasis mine.
11. Max Stackhouse, *Apologia: Contextualization, Globalization, and Mission in Theological Education* (Grand Rapids: Wm. B. Eerdmans Publishing Co., 1988), 8.
12. Farley, *Theologia.*
13. Edward Farley, *The Fragility of Knowledge: Theological Education in the Church and the University* (Philadelphia: Fortress Press, 1988).
14. Ibid., 67.
15. David H. Kelsey, *To Understand God Truly: What's Theological about a Theological School* (Louisville, Ky.: Westminster/John Knox Press, 1992).
16. Ibid., 236.
17. Iris Marion Young, *Justice and the Politics of Difference* (Princeton, N.J.: Princeton University Press, 1990), 5. See chap. 4 for a further elaboration of theology as a critical theory.
18. I must observe that, to his credit, Farley recognizes that such concrete problems do exist and that any successful conversation about theological education would have to deal with those kinds of issues. He limits himself to the ideational issues. My critique, therefore, is not with the legitimacy of his pro-

ject, which I think contributes a certain necessary type of discourse to the conversation. My critique is really a critique of addition and supplementation, intending to inquire into some concrete conditions that are necessary for the discussion in theology to be credible in present reality.

19. The 1992 Entering Student Survey conducted by the Educational Testing Service on fifty-five institutions of theological education in the United States indicated that 82 percent of all women attend seminary for "the opportunities for study and growth," while 65 percent of men "indicated this as a reason to attend seminary."

20. Farley does argue that such cultural analysis is needed. Hough and Cobb call for extensive cultural analysis in *Christian Identity and Theological Education*. My critique of their approach has to do with their failure to do an adequate cultural analysis either in terms of religious movements or crises in culture. See my essay "When the Center Cannot Contain the Margins," in *The Education of the Practical Theologian: Responses to Joseph Hough and John Cobb's "Christian Identity and Theological Education,"* ed. Don S. Browning, David Polk, and Ian S. Evison (Atlanta: Scholars Press, 1989).

21. See Robert Wuthnow, *The Restructuring of American Religion: Society and Faith since World War II* (Princeton, N.J.: Princeton University Press, 1988), 125.

22. Raymond Williams, *Marxism and Literature* (Oxford and New York: Oxford University Press, 1977), and Anthony Giddens, *The Consequences of Modernity* (Stanford, Calif.: Stanford University Press, 1990).

23. See Terry Eagleton, *The Function of Criticism: From the Spectator to Post-Structuralism* (London: Verso, 1984). Eagleton primarily addresses the function and role of literary criticism, but I am suggesting a very parallel process that goes on for theologians as they become highly specialized theological critics rather than public, constructive thinkers.

24. Alasdair MacIntyre, *After Virtue: A Study in Moral Theory* (Notre Dame, Ind.: University of Notre Dame Press, 1981).

25. Michel Foucault, *The Archaeology of Knowledge*, trans. A. M. Sheridan Smith (New York: Random House, Pantheon Books, 1972), and *Discipline and Punishment: The Birth of the Prison*, trans. Alan Sheridan (New York: Random House, 1977). See also Charles C. Lemert and Garth Gillan, *Michel Foucault: Social Theory and Transgression* (New York: Columbia University Press, 1982).

26. Kelsey, *To Understand God Truly*, 118.

27. Craig Dykstra, "Reconceiving Practice," in *Shifting Boundaries: Contextual Approaches to the Structure of Theological Education*, ed. Barbara G. Wheeler and Edward Farley (Louisville, Ky.: Westminster/John Knox Press, 1991), 35–66.

28. Kelsey, *To Understand God Truly*, 119.

29. Dykstra, "Reconceiving Practice," 50.

30. Ibid., 65. As Dykstra maintains, ordered learning must be reconceived beyond just the logical and linguistic-mathematical forms of intelligence that Farley seems to identify (and I would argue, that Kelsey agrees with, though he explicates the modern critical methods more than does Farley).

Chapter 2. Shaking the Foundations

1. See, for instance, the findings of the 1992 Entering Student Survey conducted by the Educational Testing Service, or see recent Association of Theological Schools fact books.

2. Audre Lorde, "Poetry Is Not a Luxury," in *Sister Outsider: Essays and Speeches* (Trumansburg, N.Y.: Crossing Press, 1984), 37.

3. Mary Catherine Bateson, *Composing a Life* (New York: Plume Books, 1990).
4. Toni Morrison, "Interview with Claudia Tate," in *Black Women Writers at Work,* ed. Claudia Tate (New York: Continuum, 1983), 117–31.
5. Patricia Hill Collins, *Black Feminist Thought: Knowledge, Consciousness, and the Politics of Empowerment* (New York and London: Routledge, 1990).
6. Nanette M. Roberts, "American Women and Lifestyle Change," in *Christian Feminism: Visions of a New Humanity,* ed. Judith L. Weidman (San Francisco: Harper & Row, 1984), 96.
7. Carl N. Degler, *At Odds: Women and the Family in America from the Revolution to the Present* (New York and Oxford: Oxford University Press, 1980).
8. Ibid., 418.
9. Ethel Klein, *Gender Politics: From Consciousness to Mass Politics* (Cambridge, Mass.: Harvard University Press, 1984).
10. Collins, *Black Feminist Thought,* 45.
11. Fraser's description of how women toil in the work force is worth repeating: "as feminized and sometimes sexualized 'service' workers (secretaries, domestic workers, salespersons, prostitutes, and more recently, flight attendants); as members of the helping professions utilizing mothering skills (nurses, social workers, childcare workers, primary school teachers); as targets of sexual harassment; as low-waged, low-skilled, low-status workers in sex-segregated occupations; as part-time workers; as workers who work a double shift (both unpaid domestic labor and paid labor); as 'working wives' and 'working mothers,' i.e. as primarily wives and mothers who happen, secondarily, also to 'go out to work,' as supplemental earners." Nancy Fraser, "What's Critical about Critical Theory?" in *Feminism as Critique: On the Politics of Gender,* ed. Seyla Benhabib and Drucilla Cornell (Minneapolis: University of Minnesota Press, 1987), 42–43.
12. Degler, *At Odds,* 227–48.
13. Klein, *Gender Politics,* 55.
14. Collins, *Black Feminist Thought,* 50.
15. See, for instance, Carter Heyward, *Touching Our Strength: The Erotic as Power and the Love of God* (San Francisco: Harper & Row, 1989), and Mary E. Hunt, *Fierce Tenderness: A Feminist Theology of Friendship* (New York: Crossroad, 1991).
16. For a good introduction to a variety of feminist theories, see Rosemary Tong, *Feminist Thought: A Comprehensive Introduction* (Boulder, Colo.: Westview Press, 1989).
17. Joan W. Scott, "Gender: A Useful Category of Historical Analysis," in *Coming to Terms: Feminism, Theory, Politics,* ed. Elizabeth Weed (New York: Routledge, 1989), 82.
18. Ibid., 94.
19. Ibid., 96.
20. Rebecca S. Chopp, "Situating the Structure: Prophetic Feminism and Theological Education," in *Shifting Boundaries: Contextual Approaches to the Structure of Theological Education,* ed. Barbara G. Wheeler and Edward Farley (Louisville, Ky.: Westminster/John Knox Press, 1991), 77–80.
21. See, for instance, Iris Marion Young, "Impartiality and the Civic Public: Some Implications of Feminist Critiques of Moral and Political Theory," in *Feminism as Critique,* ed. Benhabib and Cornell, 56–76.
22. Patricia Yeager, *Honey-Mad Women: Emancipatory Strategies in Women's Writings* (New York: Columbia University Press, 1988).
23. Susan Faludi, *Backlash: The Undeclared War against American Women* (New York: Crown Publishers, 1991).
24. Sidonie Smith, *A Poetics of Women's Autobiography: Marginality and the Fictions*

of Self-Representation (Bloomington and Indianapolis: Indiana University Press, 1987), 38.

25. Carolyn G. Heilbrun, *Writing a Woman's Life* (New York and London: W. W. Norton and Co., 1988), 27–31.

26. Collins, *Black Feminist Thought*, 70–78.

27. Yeager, *Honey-Mad Women*, 6.

28. Tate, *Black Women Writers at Work*, xxiv. See also Barbara Christian, *Black Feminist Criticism, Perspectives on Black Women Writers* (New York: Pergamon Press, 1985).

29. Alasdair MacIntyre, *After Virtue: A Study in Moral Theory* (Notre Dame, Ind.: University of Notre Dame Press, 1981).

30. David Carr, *Time, Narrative, and History* (Bloomington and Indianapolis: Indiana University Press, 1986).

31. With the decentering, if not demise, of foundationalism and universalism of liberal reason, more and more philosophers turn to narrativity to examine a kind of decentered subject, decentered within traditions and social relations, and decentered in the sense of never completely fixed.

32. Ibid., 70.

33. Stephen Crites, "The Narrative Quality of Experience," *Journal of the American Academy of Religion* 39 (1971): 291–331.

34. Hans Frei, *The Eclipse of Biblical Narrative* (New Haven, Conn.: Yale University Press, 1974).

35. David Tracy, *The Analogical Imagination: Christian Theology and the Culture of Pluralism* (New York: Crossroad, 1981).

36. Smith, *A Poetics*, 38.

37. Two extremes are worth avoiding: one having to do with merely fitting into already determined narratives, the other having to do with interpretations of narratives to mirror already experienced states of consciousness. Notions of "submission" to biblical narratives tend to deny the agency and responsibility of my own narrativity and tempt us to think that narratives are fixed and not read anew in many different ways and times. Notions of "interpreting" the narratives by bracketing the situatedness of the interpreter tend to remove the practical intent of narratives.

38. The notion of writing a woman's life has been made popular by Heilbrun in *Writing a Woman's Life.*

39. Valerie Saiving, "The Human Situation: A Feminine View," in *Womanspirit Rising: A Feminist Reader in Religion,* ed. Carol P. Christ and Judith Plaskow (San Francisco: Harper & Row, 1970), 25.

40. Rosemary Radford Ruether, *Sexism and God-Talk: Toward a Feminist Theology* (Boston: Beacon Press, 1983).

41. Nelle Morton, *The Journey Is Home* (Boston: Beacon Press, 1985), 55.

42. The term *experience* is itself a word that needs some attention, especially as a space for narrativity. "Experience" in much modern theology functioned as a way to get at the universal, most "fundamental," and, supposedly, the common structure of our experience. But, as Saiving and other feminists pointed out, often the experience of one group—white, middle-class Eurocentric men—was lifted up as universal. So feminists turned to the term *experience* not as what we share in an abstract way, but what one has in a particular and concrete fashion: e.g., my particular experiences. Experience is a space to explore the lived realities of social constructs as well as one's own individual agency, emotions, transcendence. As a space for the exploration of narrative, experience does not "authorize" narrativity as much as it provides material in need of explanation, reflection, transformation.

43. Jacqueline Grant, *White Women's Christ and Black Women's Jesus: Feminist Christology and Womanist Response* (Atlanta: Scholars Press, 1989).

44. Chung Hyun Kyung, *Struggle to Be the Sun Again: Introducing Asian Women's Theology* (Maryknoll, N.Y.: Orbis Books, 1990).

45. Ada María Isasi-Díaz, "Toward an Understanding of *Feminismo Hispano* in the U.S.A.," *Women's Consciousness, Women's Conscience: A Reader in Feminist Ethics*, ed. Barbara Hilkert Andolsen, Christine E. Gudorf, and Mary A. Pellauer (Minneapolis: Seabury Press, 1985), 59.

46. Janet Ruth Jakobsen, *The Gendered Division of Moral Labor and the Possibilities of a Responsible Feminist Ethic* (Ph.D. diss., Emory University, 1992), 19.

47. Elizabeth V. Spelman, *Inessential Woman: Problems of Exclusion in Feminist Thought* (Boston: Beacon Press, 1988).

48. See Linda Alcoff, "Cultural Feminism versus Post-Structuralism: The Identity Crisis in Feminist Theory," *Signs: Journal of Women in Culture and Society* 13 (1988): 433.

49. Barbara Patterson, correspondence, May 5, 1994.

50. Elisabeth Schüssler Fiorenza, *Bread Not Stone: The Challenge of Feminist Biblical Interpretation* (Boston: Beacon Press, 1986).

51. Rebecca S. Chopp, *The Power to Speak: Feminism, Language, God* (New York: Crossroad, 1989).

52. MacIntyre, *After Virtue*, 178.

53. Katie G. Cannon, *Black Womanist Ethics* (Atlanta: Scholars Press, 1988).

54. Ibid., 5–6.

55. Beverly Wildung Harrison, "The Power of Anger in the Work of Love: Christian Ethics for Women and Other Strangers," in *Making the Connections: Essays in Feminist Social Ethics*, ed. Carol S. Robb (Boston: Beacon Press, 1985), 11. Harrison refers to "basepoints" for what I am calling virtues.

56. Ruth L. Smith, "Feminism and the Moral Subject," in *Women's Consciousness, Women's Conscience*, 250.

57. Maxine Greene, *The Dialectic of Freedom* (New York and London: Teachers College Press, 1988), 22.

58. Edward Farley, *The Fragility of Knowledge: Theological Education in the Church and University* (Philadelphia: Fortress Press, 1988), 74–79.

Chapter 3. Places of Grace

1. Elisabeth Schüssler Fiorenza, *Discipleship of Equals: A Critical Feminist Ekklesia-logy of Liberation* (New York: Crossroad, 1993). The question of what to call the church within feminist liberation Christianity is an interesting and complex one. Though *women-church* has been popular, I prefer *the ekklesia. Women-church* is an excellent term for subversion, since it immediately claims the term *church* for women's experiences within Christianity, something long ignored. On the other hand, the term *women* tends to tempt exclusionary practices of "other" women and of men, which is neither the reality nor the desire of church within feminist liberation Christianity. As Schüssler Fiorenza has developed it, the term *ekklesia* most aptly names what I understand this practice to be about. Though Schüssler Fiorenza also uses the term *ekkelsia-logy*, I have kept with the traditional term, *ecclesiology*, both for linguistic convenience and by way of claiming that feminist discourse on the ekklesia continues the classical tradition of reflection on the doctrine of ecclesiology.

2. Joseph C. Hough, Jr., and John B. Cobb, Jr., *Christian Identity and Theological Education* (Chico, Calif.: Scholars Press, 1985), 4.

3. David Kelsey, *To Understand God Truly: What's Theological about a Theological School* (Louisville, Ky.: Westminster/John Knox Press, 1992).
4. H. Richard Niebuhr in collaboration with Daniel Day Williams and James M. Gustafson, *The Purpose of the Church and Its Ministry: Reflections on the Aims of Theological Education* (New York: Harper & Row, 1956), 17–18.
5. Peter C. Hodgson, *Revisioning the Church: Ecclesial Freedom in the New Paradigm* (Philadelphia: Fortress Press, 1988), 64.
6. Jürgen Moltmann, *Theology of Hope: On the Ground and the Implications of a Christian Eschatology* (San Francisco: Harper & Row, 1967), and Johannes Baptist Metz, *The Emergent Church: The Future of Christianity in a Postbourgeois World*, trans. Peter Mann (New York: Crossroad, 1981).
7. I am using the method of portraiture developed by Edward Farley in *Ecclesial Reflection: An Anatomy of Theological Method* (Philadelphia: Fortress Press, 1982) and extended to emphasize cultural diversity and political dynamics by Mark Kline Taylor in his *Remembering Esperanza: A Cultural-Political Theology for North American Praxis* (Maryknoll, N.Y.: Orbis Books, 1990).
8. Anne E. Carr, *Transforming Grace: Christian Tradition and Women's Experience* (San Francisco: Harper & Row, 1988).
9. The literature on paradigm change and Christianity is vast. See, for instance, *Paradigm Change in Theology: A Symposium for the Future*, ed. Hans Küng and David Tracy, trans. Margaret Kohl (New York: Crossroad, 1989). In a great deal of the literature theologians often seem to treat paradigm change as simply the transformation of ideas. Historically, however, paradigm change is connected with transformations in practices and institutions.
10. Rita Nakashima Brock, *Journeys by Heart: A Christology of Erotic Power* (New York: Crossroad, 1988), 70.
11. Elisabeth Schüssler Fiorenza tells this story in *But She Said: Feminist Practices of Biblical Interpretation* (Boston: Beacon Press, 1992), 127. For a more extensive treatment of Schüssler Fiorenza's experiences in and reflection on the ekklesia, see her *Discipleship of Equals*.
12. Mary Ann Zimmer, "Faith and Practice in the Everyday: A Critical Resource for the Transformation of Theology" (Ph.D. diss., Emory University, in process).
13. This is a common move in Christian theology. See, for instance, Jürgen Moltmann, *The Church in the Power of the Spirit: A Contribution to Messianic Ecclesiology*, trans. Margaret Kohl (San Francisco: Harper & Row, 1977).
14. Schüssler Fiorenza, *But She Said*, 128.
15. Friedrich Schleiermacher, *The Christian Faith*, 2d ed., ed. H. R. Mackintosh and J. S. Stewart (Philadelphia: Fortress Press, 1968), 358.
16. Avery Dulles, S.J., *Models of the Church* (Garden City, N.Y.: Doubleday & Co., 1978), 67–79.
17. Gustavo Gutiérrez, *A Theology of Liberation*, trans. and ed. Caridad Inda and John Eagleson (Maryknoll, N.Y.: Orbis Books, 1973), 260.
18. Sallie McFague, *The Body of God: An Ecological Theology* (Minneapolis: Fortress Press, 1993), 206.
19. See, for instance, Mary Potter Engel, "Evil, Sin, and Violation of the Vulnerable," in *Lift Every Voice: Constructing Christian Theologies from the Underside*, ed. Susan Brooks Thistlethwaite and Mary Potter Engel (San Francisco: Harper & Row, 1990), 152–64.
20. Elisabeth Schüssler Fiorenza, "The Politics of Otherness: Biblical Interpretation as a Critical Praxis for Liberation," in *Expanding the View: Gustavo Gutiérrez and the Future of Liberation Theology*, ed. Marc H. Ellis and Otto Madura (Maryknoll, N.Y.: Orbis Books, 1988), 140.

21. Marge Piercy, "Rape poem," *Circles on the Water: Selected Poems of Marge Piercy* (New York: Alfred A. Knopf, 1990), 164.

22. Toni Morrison, *The Bluest Eye* (New York: Washington Square Press, 1970), 158. I am indebted to Engel for this quotation in her superb article on rape, evil, and sin: "Evil, Sin, and Violation," 152–64.

23. See Rebecca S. Chopp, "Feminism and the Theology of Sin," *The Ecumenist* 1, no. 1 (Nov.–Dec. 1993): 12–16.

24. Rosemary Radford Ruether, *Women-Church: Theology and Practice of Feminist Liturgical Communities* (San Francisco: Harper & Row, 1985), 154.

25. McFague, *The Body of God,* and Pamela D. Couture, *Blessed Are the Poor? Women's Poverty, Family Policy, and Practical Theology* (Nashville: Abingdon Press, 1991).

26. Delores S. Williams, *Sisters in the Wilderness: The Challenge of Womanist God-Talk* (Maryknoll, N.Y.: Orbis Books, 1993).

27. Paul Tillich, *Systematic Theology,* 3 vols. (Chicago: University of Chicago Press, 1951–63), 2:29.

28. I am influenced in my understanding of this depth ordering by Patricia Hill Collins, *Black Feminist Thought: Knowledge, Consciousness, and the Politics of Empowerment* (London: Routledge, 1990), and Joan Cocks, *The Oppositional Imagination: Feminism, Critique, and Political Theory* (London and New York: Routledge, 1989).

29. For a parallel use of the term *idolatry,* see Gustavo Gutiérrez, *The God of Life,* trans. Matthew J. O'Connell (Maryknoll, N.Y.: Orbis Books, 1991).

30. Schüssler Fiorenza, *But She Said,* 6–7.

31. Metz, *The Emergent Church.*

32. Robin Lovin, "Justice," in *A New Handbook of Christian Theology,* ed. Donald W. Musser and Joseph L. Price (Nashville: Abingdon Press, 1992), 266.

33. Iris Marion Young, *Justice and the Politics of Difference* (Princeton, N.J.: Princeton University Press, 1990).

34. Ibid., 34.

35. Ibid., 39.

36. Schüssler Fiorenza, *Bread Not Stone* (Boston: Beacon Press, 1986), 7.

37. See, for instance, Nancy Fraser, "Rethinking the Public Sphere: A Contribution to the Critique of Actually Existing Democracy," in *Social Text* 25, no. 6 (1990): 56–80.

38. Michael J. Sandel, *Liberalism and the Limits of Justice* (Cambridge: Cambridge University Press, 1982), 140–48.

39. Letty M. Russell, *Household of Freedom: Authority in Feminist Theology* (Philadelphia: Westminster Press, 1987).

40. Pamela M. Hall, *Narrative and the Natural Law: An Interpretation of Thomist Ethics* (Notre Dame, Ind.: University of Notre Dame Press, forthcoming in 1994).

41. Thomas Aquinas, *Summa theologica,* 1a–2ae. q.65, a.5, resp.

42. McFague, *Body of God,* 112.

43. Nancy Eiesland has continued her sermon in a book: *The Disabled God: Toward a Liberatory Theology of Disability* (Nashville: Abingdon Press, 1994).

44. Karl Rahner, *Foundations of Christian Faith: An Introduction to the Idea of Christianity,* trans. William V. Dych (New York: Crossroad, 1978).

45. Peter C. Hodgson, *Winds of the Spirit: A Constructive Christian Theology* (Louisville, Ky.: Westminster/John Knox Press, 1994), 204–8.

46. Susan Brooks Thistlethwaite, *Sex, Race, and God: Christian Feminism in Black and White* (New York: Crossroad, 1989).

47. See Rebecca S. Chopp, "Feminism's Theological Pragmatics: A Social Naturalism of Women's Experience," *Journal of Religion* 67 (April 1987): 239–56.
48. For two contemporary formulations of naturalism, see P. F. Strawson, *Skepticism and Naturalism: Some Varieties* (New York: Columbia University Press, 1985), and Morton White, *What Is and Ought to Be Done: An Essay in Ethics and Epistemology* (New York: Oxford University Press, 1981).
49. Fumitaka Matsuoka, "Pluralism at Home: Globalization within North America," *Theological Education* 26 (Spring 1990), Supplement 1: 39–40.
50. The Mud Flower Collective, *God's Fierce Whimsy: Christian Feminism and Theological Education* (New York: Pilgrim Press, 1985), 204.
51. Sharon Welch, "An Ethics of Solidarity and Difference," in *Postmodernism, Feminism, and Cultural Politics: Redrawing Educational Boundaries*, ed. Henry A. Giroux (Albany: State University of New York Press, 1991), 88–89.
52. Elisabeth Schüssler Fiorenza, "The Will to Choose or Reject: Continuing Our Critical Work," in *Feminist Interpretation of the Bible*, ed. Letty M. Russell (Philadelphia: Westminster Press, 1985), 134–35; Brock, *Journeys by Heart.*

Chapter 4: The Warming Quilt of God

1. Megan Beverly, "Preaching from a Feminist Perspective: 'A Crazy Quilt'" (manuscript, 1992), 2–3. Used by permission.
2. See Elaine Showalter, "Piecing and Writing," in *The Poetics of Gender*, ed. Nancy K. Miller (New York: Columbia University Press, 1986), 223, and Judith Plaskow and Carol P. Christ, eds., *Weaving the Visions: New Patterns in Feminist Spirituality* (San Francisco: Harper & Row, 1989).
3. Elisabeth Schüssler Fiorenza, "The 'Quilting' of Women's History: Phoebe of Cenchreae," in *Embodied Love: Sensuality and Relationship as Feminist Values*, ed. Paula M. Cooey, Sharon A. Farmer, and Mary Ellen Ross (San Francisco: Harper & Row, 1987), 35–49.
4. See the definition of *praxis* offered by Langdon Gilkey, *Reaping the Whirlwind: A Christian Interpretation of History* (New York: Seabury Press, 1976), 69. See also Rebecca S. Chopp, "Praxis," *New Dictionary of Catholic Spirituality*, ed. Michael Downey (Collegeville, Minn.: Liturgical Press, 1993), 756–64.
5. Catherine Keller, "Piling Up and Hopefully Saving: Eschatology as a Feminist Problem" (paper presented to the Work Group on Constructive Theology, October 1989), 10. Quoted in Peter C. Hodgson, *Winds of the Spirit: A Constructive Christian Theology* (Louisville, Ky.: Westminster/John Knox Press, 1994), 39–40.
6. Edward Farley, *The Fragility of Knowledge: Theological Education in the Church and the University* (Philadelphia: Fortress Press, 1988), 22.
7. Both David Kelsey and Robert Schreiter have recently suggested various models of theology. Kelsey suggests that understanding in Christian theology has included the models of wisdom, theoria, knowledge through the affections, and as action or praxis. Schreiter identifies four approaches of theology as variations in a sacred text, as wisdom, as sure knowledge, and as praxis. Feminist theology, within both topologies, would be characterized as a type of praxis. See especially chap. 2, "Crossroad Hamlets," in David Kelsey, *To Understand God Truly: What's Theological about a Theological School* (Louisville, Ky.: Westminster/John Knox Press, 1992), 30–62, and Robert J. Schreiter, *Constructing Local Theologies* (Maryknoll, N.Y.: Orbis Books, 1985), 80–93.
8. Cornel West, *The American Evasion of Philosophy: A Genealogy of Pragmatism* (Madison: University of Wisconsin Press, 1989).

9. Ibid., 5.

10. Ibid., 230.

11. In so doing, the critical theorist can be spoken of as a *bricoleur,* a kind of handy-person who brings together imagination, skill, and resources in addressing particular concrete problems. Following Jeffrey Stout, I want to use this term from anthropologist Claude Lévi-Strauss to describe the theologian and her work. Jeffrey Stout, *Ethics after Babel: The Languages of Morals and Their Discontents* (Boston: Beacon Press, 1988).

12. Mark C. Taylor, *Erring: A Postmodern A/theology* (Chicago: University of Chicago Press, 1984).

13. Peter C. Hodgson, *Winds of the Spirit: A Constructive Christian Theology* (Louisville, Ky.: Westminster/John Knox Press, 1994), 63.

14. Taylor, *Erring,* 6.

15. Ibid., 15.

16. David Tracy, *The Analogical Imagination: Christian Theology and the Culture of Pluralism* (New York: Crossroad, 1981).

17. Ibid., 145 n. 75. Quoted in Werner G. Jeanrod, *Text and Interpretation as Categories of Theological Thinking,* trans. Thomas J. Wilson (New York: Crossroad, 1988), 138.

18. George A. Lindbeck, *The Nature of Doctrine: Religion and Theology in a Post-Liberal Age* (Philadelphia: Westminster Press, 1984).

19. Ronald F. Thiemann, *Revelation and Theology: The Gospel as Narrated Promise* (Notre Dame, Ind.: University of Notre Dame Press, 1985), 75.

20. William C. Placher, *Unapologetic Theology: A Christian Voice in a Pluralistic Conversation* (Louisville, Ky.: Westminster/John Knox Press, 1989), 161.

21. Raymond Geuss, *The Idea of a Critical Theory* (Cambridge: Cambridge University Press, 1981), 2.

22. For an extended argument concerning the need for aesthetical reimaging of language in relation to politics, see Fred Dallymar, *Language and Politics: Why Does Language Matter to Political Philosophy?* (Notre Dame, Ind.: University of Notre Dame Press, 1984).

23. Schreiter, *Constructing Local Theologies.*

24. Rita Nakashima Brock, *Journeys by Heart: A Christology of Erotic Power* (New York: Crossroad, 1988).

25. Jacquelyn Grant, *White Women's Christ and Black Women's Jesus: Feminist Christology and Womanist Response* (Atlanta: Scholars Press, 1989).

26. Rosemary Radford Ruether, *Sexism and God-Talk: Toward a Feminist Theology* (Boston: Beacon Press, 1983).

27. For this critical construction of symbols, see Rebecca S. Chopp, *The Praxis of Suffering: An Interpretation of Liberation and Political Theologies* (Maryknoll, N.Y.: Orbis Books, 1986), 142–44. My approach is a cultural-political appropriation of Tillich's famous notion of Catholic substance and the Protestant principle.

28. Elizabeth A. Johnson, *She Who Is: The Mystery of God in Feminist Theological Discourse* (New York: Crossroad, 1992), 4.

29. Mary Daly, *Beyond God the Father: Toward a Philosophy of Women's Liberation* (Boston: Beacon Press, 1973), 19.

30. Marcia Falk, "Notes on Composing New Blessings," in *Weaving the Visions,* ed. Plaskow and Christ, 128–38.

31. Carter Heyward, *The Redemption of God: A Theology of Mutual Relation* (Washington, D.C.: University Press of America, 1982), and *Touching Our Strength: The Erotic as Power and the Love of God* (San Francisco: Harper & Row, 1989).

32. Susan Brooks Thistlethwaite, "Every Two Minutes: Battered Women and Feminist Interpretation," in *Feminist Interpretation of the Bible*, ed. Letty M. Russell (Philadelphia: Westminster Press, 1985), 96–110.

33. Sallie McFague, *Models of God: Theology for an Ecological, Nuclear Age* (Philadelphia: Fortress Press, 1987).

34. Rebecca S. Chopp, *The Power to Speak: Feminism, Language, God* (New York: Crossroad, 1989), 138.

35. Marjorie Procter-Smith, *In Her Own Rite: Constructing Feminist Liturgical Tradition* (Nashville: Abingdon Press, 1990), 37.

36. Johnson, *She Who Is*, 71.

37. Sally Purvis, "Christian Feminist Spirituality," in *Christian Spirituality: Post-Reformation and Modern*, ed. Louis Dupré and Don Saliers (New York: Crossroad, 1989), 509.

38. Johnson, *She Who Is*, 233.

39. Jacqueline Grant, *White Women's Christ and Black Women's Jesus: Feminist Christology and Womanist Response* (Atlanta: Scholars Press, 1989).

40. See, for instance, Heyward, *Touching Our Strength*, 99.

41. Rosemary Radford Ruether, *Women-Church: Theology and Practice of Feminist Liturgical Communities* (San Francisco: Harper & Row, 1985).

42. Elisabeth Schüssler Fiorenza, *Discipleship of Equals: A Critical Feminist Ekklesialogy of Liberation* (New York: Crossroad, 1993).

43. Sallie McFague, *The Body of God: An Ecological Theology* (Minneapolis: Fortress Press, 1993), 211.

44. Jane Tompkins, ed., *Reader-Response Criticism: From Formalism to Post-Structuralism* (Baltimore and London: John Hopkins Press, 1980).

45. Don Compier, "Sin, Calvin, and the Rhetorical Tradition" (Ph.D. diss., Emory University, 1991), 82.

46. Terry Eagleton, *Against the Grain: Selected Essays* (London: Verso, 1986), 169.

47. M. E. Hawkesworth, *Beyond Oppression: Feminist Theory and Political Strategy* (New York: Continuum, 1990), 111.

48. Schüssler Fiorenza, "The 'Quilting' of Women's History," 35–50.

49. Elisabeth Schüssler Fiorenza, *But She Said: Feminist Practices of Biblical Interpretation* (Boston: Beacon Press, 1992), 131–32.

50. Ibid., 132.

51. Ibid.

52. Beverly, "Preaching from a Feminist Perspective," 3.

53. Ibid.

Chapter 5. A Particular Vision

1. For a brief argument about this notion of how ideas function in different models, see Ann Swidler, "Culture in Action: Symbols and Strategies," in *American Sociological Review* 51 (1986): 273–86.

2. In my experience, this fact is often overlooked by many in theology and theological education. For any number of reasons that could bear careful scrutiny, many today do not want to inquire into feminist practices, but rather merely to consider part of feminism's ideas in relation to other sets of ideas. We must ask such persons to become bicultural and bilingual, for it is necessary in order to understand feminist theological practices to surround oneself with them and then to understand the ideas and symbols from within the practices.

3. Recall David Kelsey's argument: "Out of *praxis* that aims at transforming oppressive social power arrangements arise fresh theoretical understandings of the structure and dynamics of oppressive relationships within society." *To Understand God Truly: What's Theological about a Theological School* (Louisville, Ky.: Westminster/John Knox Press, 1992), 48.

4. Craig Dykstra, "Reconceiving Practice," in *Shifting Boundaries: Contextual Approaches to the Structure of Theological Education,* ed. Barbara G. Wheeler and Edward Farley (Louisville, Ky.: Westminster/John Knox Press, 1991), 65–66.

5. Ibid.

6. Actually Kelsey never really explains how he thinks *habitus* and critical thinking of the modern type can be combined. After affirming that the goal of theological education ought to be "Athens" (his code for Farley's goal of *theologia*), he argues that the actual type of reflection will be that of Berlin (his code for modern reflective thought). "A theological school according to this utopian proposal would appropriate from 'Berlin' an openness to take as its subject of study *all* components of the Christian thing concretely present in and as congregations, their social and institutional forms as well as their texts and their forms and contents. It would also appropriate from 'Berlin' its disciplines of critical and self-critical inquiry that assume nothing is exempt from critical testing. However, it would appropriate these aspects of the 'Berlin' model of excellent schooling by abstracting them from the institutional structures that make them the concrete practices they are in research universities. Thus, in its concrete reality such a theological school would no more consist of the institutionalized practices constituting an actual school modeled on 'Berlin' than it would consist of the institutionalized practices constituting an actual school modeled on 'Athens.' It would simply be itself." It is this "being itself" that is never explicated, though Kelsey's book offers some rich promises about how it might be understood. Kelsey, *To Understand God Truly,* 236–37.

7. Dykstra, "Reconceiving Practice."

8. Mary Field Belenky, Blythe McVicker Clinchy, Nancy Rule Goldberger, and Jill Mattuck Tarule, *Women's Ways of Knowing: The Development of Self, Voice, and Mind* (New York: Basic Books, 1986).

9. Patricia Hill Collins, *Black Feminist Thought: Knowledge, Consciousness and the Politics of Empowerment* (New York and London: Routledge, 1990), 206–20.

10. Susan J. Hekman, *Gender and Knowledge: Elements of a Postmodern Feminism* (Boston: Northeastern University Press, 1990).

11. The Mud Flower Collective, *God's Fierce Whimsy: Christian Feminism and Theological Education* (New York: Pilgrim Press, 1985), 204. Given the argument of this book in terms of how ideas relate to practices, I would rephrase this sentence to read: "the fundamental process of theological education must be the doing of justice."

12. Elisabeth Schüssler Fiorenza, "Theological Education: Biblical Studies," in *The Education of the Practical Theologian: Responses to Joseph Hough and John Cobb's Christian Identity and Theological Education,* ed. Don S. Browning, David Polk, and Ian S. Evison (Atlanta: Scholars Press, 1989), 18–19.

13. Sharon Welch, "An Ethic of Solidarity and Difference," in *Postmodernism, Feminism, and Cultural Politics: Redrawing Educational Boundaries* (Albany: State University of New York Press), 83–99.

14. Ibid., 93.

15. Maxine Greene, *The Dialectic of Freedom* (New York: Teachers College Press, 1988), 5.

16. For a notion of reason as communicative and dialogic, see Peter Hodgson, *Winds of the Spirit: A Constructive Christian Theology* (Louisville, Ky.: Westminster/John Knox, 1994), 99.

17. For David Tracy's most extensive treatment of conversation, see his *The Analogical Imagination: Christian Theology and the Culture of Pluralism* (New York: Crossroad, 1981).

18. For a parallel argument about the problem with abstract or universal selfs who forget all particularities, see Seyla Benhabib, "The Generalized Other and the Concrete Other: The Kohlberg-Gilligan Controversy and Feminist Theory," in *Feminism as Critique: On the Politics of Gender*, ed. Seyla Benhabib and Drucilla Cornell (Minneapolis: University of Minnesota Press, 1987), 77–95.

19. Hodgson, *Winds of the Spirit*, 99.

20. Iris Marion Young, *Justice and the Politics of Difference* (Princeton, N.J.: Princeton University Press, 1990), 6.

21. Marjorie Procter-Smith, *In Her Own Rite: Constructing Feminist Liturgical Tradition* (Nashville: Abingdon Press, 1990), 37.

22. Charles M. Wood, *Vision and Discernment: An Orientation in Theological Study* (Atlanta: Scholars Press, 1985). See also Rebecca S. Chopp, "Emerging Issues and Theological Education," *Theological Education* 26, no. 2 (Spring 1990): 118–22.

23. Ibid., 23.

24. Fumitaka Matsuoka, "Pluralism at Home: Globalization within North America," *Theological Education* 26 (Spring 1990), Supplement I: 39–40.

25. Greene, *Dialectic of Freedom*, 22.

26. For an excellent essay on attending to cultural problematics in theological education, see Mark Kline Taylor, "Celebrating Difference, Resisting Domination: The Need for Synchronic Strategies in Theological Education," in *Shifting Boundaries*, ed. Wheeler and Farley, 259–94.

27. John Dewey, *Democracy and Education* (New York: Macmillan Co., 1916).

28. Clifford Geertz, *The Interpretation of Cultures: Selected Essays* (New York: Basic Books, 1973), 7–10. I am indebted to Charles R. Foster and Theodore Brelsford for expanding on Geertz's notion in terms of the congregation in their *We Are the Church Together: Cultural Diversity in Forming Congregational Life* (manuscript, Emory University, 1993).

29. Gail B. Griffin, *Calling: Essays on Teaching in the Mother Tongue* (Pasadena, Calif.: Trilogy Books, 1992).

30. Lewis Carroll, *Alice's Adventures in Wonderland* (New York: Harper, 1901), 93–94.

31. Elisabeth Schüssler Fiorenza, *But She Said: Feminist Practices of Biblical Interpretation* (Boston: Beacon Press, 1992), 180.

32. Ibid., 185.

Index